P**raise**

"*How to Be a DIVA at Public Speaking* is truly an inspirational book full of ready-to-implement tips and guidance in order for you to become a confident star on stage. Shola has developed a unique, highly effective and easy-to-understand system to master public speaking. I cannot wait to transform my speeches and presentations into high-impact, engaging and authentic performances! I already feel like a DIVA. Thank you Shola for such a valuable book that I'm sure many will find motivating and uplifting." **Saija Mahon, Founder CEO of Mahon Digital Marketing Ltd**

"This book by Ms Kaye is invaluable and came at a pivotal point in my career. Even though I have been teaching and speaking for over 30 years I learned an amazing amount of new approaches. There are so many well thought out tools to improve speaking skills, confidence levels, and more. I wasn't disappointed at all with this book. In fact, I implemented her teachings right away in the class I was teaching this weekend and wowed my students." **Wendy Van de Poll, MS, CEOL**

"I've been speaking professionally since 2009 and I found this book to be a credible and valuable resource. I appreciated how the author wove in stories to illustrate her points. So many great and actionable take-aways. I hope fellow members of the National Speakers Association get their hands on this book, especially those just getting started as professional speakers." **Robbie Samuels, Professional Speaker**

"How many of us have sung our hearts out in front of the mirror with a hair brush in hand listening to the crowds explode in applause as you gave the performance of your life? As a singer for over 30 years, I LOVED how Shola paralleled singing with public speaking. She teaches how to channel your inner pop DIVA to get your message across in exciting ways. She illustrates her points with creative analogies to show how fun getting in front of an audience and speaking to them can be. She gives you step-by-step instructions on what to do before, during and after your presentation. You will discover your DIVA style and embrace it to your best ability. This book was a joy to read. The author weaved in many great stories that helped keep my attention the entire time (which is hard to do). I guarantee, after reading it, you will be able to take your presentation from dull to show-stopping. Your audience is waiting. Break a leg!" **Julie Carruth, Author**

"Shola offered our start-ups a fantastic workshop exploring the art of presenting confidently which really showed at the demo day pitches at the end of our cohort. Her experience as a singer was invaluable and showed how skills can be easily transferred across into the business world. The workshop was highly engaging and the start-ups came out full of energy, a new found confidence and had vastly improved their pitch." **Rishi Chowdhury, Founder, Incubus Ventures**

"Shola came and spoke to our Amway Business Owners and gave us an inspirational talk on the subject of Finding Your Voice. We were amazed that someone who used to hide in meetings for fear of speaking up could deliver a presentation with such presence and command such attention – all due to her highly engaging delivery style. Shola kept us engaged with her voice, her body and her story. We were carried on her journey with such detail as if we were part of it ourselves." **Maxine Gabriel, Amway Education Manager, UK & ROI**

"I have been pretty nervous about my first public speaking gig and felt I needed a helping hand with planning and advice. Thank goodness I found this book! I have highlighted so many sections on my Kindle that I will refer back to. Not only was there a load of helpful advice, but I also really enjoyed Shola's writing style. It felt a bit like chatting with an encouraging friend (well a friend who knows a whole lot about public speaking). I now feel so much more confident about my talk and can't wait to put what I have learnt into practice." **Catherine, Amazon Customer**

"The thought of public speaking has always made my blood run cold, but it's something I know I need to learn how to do. I had no idea where to start until I read this book . . . even just one chapter in I was imagining myself on stage and loving it! This book tells you exactly how to deliver to an audience in a really engaging, entertaining way. The author really walks her talk and I can't thank her enough for all of the tips and invaluable advice it contains." **Leslie Beattie, Amazon Customer**

HOW TO BE A DIVA AT PUBLIC SPEAKING

The Step-by-Step System to Engage Your Audience and Present with Confidence

Shola Kaye

How to be a DIVA at Public Speaking: The step-by-step system to engage your audience and present with confidence

By Shola Kaye

ISBN: 978-1-5136-2034-3

Definition and Dedication

DIVA: Italian, literally goddess, from Latin, feminine of divus divine, god (Merriam Webster)

To all the women reading this book: you don't need to be rich, famous or glamorous to be a DIVA.

Acknowledgements

A huge thank you goes to George, my sweet pea. Your endless patience and belief in me made this book possible.

Thanks also to the team at Self-Publishing School for all your support and encouragement.

Cheers to Nieal Grewal of Click UK Ltd for her cover design idea, and to Lizette Balsdon for her editing skills.

Thanks to my sister for your detailed knowledge and advice.

Big thanks also to Andrew, you showed me the joy of reading poetry and helped me believe I could become an award-winning speaker.

Thank you to coach Rasheed Ogunlaru who suggested I write this book before any other.

To Sue Austin for being a big fan and to Jill, Suzi and Sarah for your helpful suggestions. To my wonderful foster mother Irene Grace, who showed endless love and generosity. You supported me every step of the way.

To my parents for your love.

To all the DIVAs out there who have attended my programmes, thanks for putting your trust in me!

Table of Contents

Read This First!

To help you get the most out of this book I've created a number of FREE resources. For your convenience, all can be found at sholakaye.com/divabookcourse and will be delivered as an online course.

You will have FREE access to:

- A downloadable audio book that will retail for approximately £19.99 on Audible. By signing up for the online course I will be able to notify you as soon as it's ready.

- A concise video course consisting of a 1-2 minute overview of each chapter in the book and demonstrations of breathing and voice exercises.

- A downloadable PDF workbook with exercises and checklists to accompany some of the book's chapters.

- An audio visualisation exercise. Use this to overcome nerves and create a mindset of public speaking success.

Would you please help?

If you enjoy this book, will you **please go to your local Amazon store and leave a brief review?**

That way even more people can become DIVAs at public speaking!

Use http://getbook.at/diva to go straight to your local Amazon online store.

Introduction

Before we plunge into the tips, tools, and techniques that will help you unlock your inner DIVA speaker, let's look at why you should read this book, who this book is for, what inspired me to write it, and how to use it.

Why Read This Book?

If I asked you to create a speech, would you be flustered and anxious, or excited and enthusiastic? Many would see it as a huge, long-winded task. The delivery of the speech would be a whole other issue. Worries about coping with nerves, stage-fright, what to do with your hands, and much more, might well pop up.

I could recommend that you study Dr. Martin Luther King's *I have a dream* speech (sholakaye.com/ihaveadream). You could watch a YouTube clip of Michelle Obama (sholakaye.com/obama) or even one of Margaret Thatcher (sholakaye.com/thatcher), to find out how it's done. For most people, however, it's pretty difficult to break down the key elements of what makes a speech—or a speaker—great, and then apply those lessons to their own work. Besides that, it's better to be brilliant versions of ourselves than a poor version of someone else. We need to find ways to develop our own style.

As speakers we can learn a lot from the performances of top pop singers. They work the stage in their own unique way. They hold our attention. Their songs have emotional highs and lows that keep us gripped, coupled with catchy lyrics that we remember easily, sometimes even after hearing only once.

More importantly, we've been listening to pop songs since we were little kids. How could we avoid them?

They were played on the radio, on TV, we chatted about them at school. And we watched singers perform. Even if we couldn't get to gigs and shows, we would see them on TV. We'd notice that some artists always sang ballads and didn't move around much; that others paced up and down the stage like caged animals and were full of energy. We'd realise that we liked some songs more than others and it was OK. We didn't need to go deep and analyse how many times the lead singer sang the song title, or where she stood to deliver the verse and the chorus. We just watched, absorbed and enjoyed.

In this book, I will draw parallels between pop DIVAs and their songs vs. public speaking and speeches. These analogies and references will help you see that public speaking can be fun and accessible. That it doesn't have to be an intellectual activity. That you can apply a few simple techniques that you most likely already know from watching YouTube, MTV, or Top of the Pops, and those techniques will lift the quality of your public speaking ten-fold.

Also, it's rare for people to aspire to be great public speakers from a young age, but most of us, at some point or another, have pretended to be a pop DIVA.

I'd like you to recapture that playful energy, the spirit of adventure and abandon that comes with grasping a hairbrush, a vacuum cleaner handle, or a Coke bottle and pretending you're on stage with thousands of fans calling out your name.

Here are some of the many similarities between public speaking and singing. Both speakers and singers may need to:

- Warm up the audience

- Form a bond with the audience

- Work the stage

- Craft a chorus or 'throughline'

- Build in highs and lows

- Create intimate moments

- Be vulnerable

- Get the audience to buy 'stuff'—whether that be ideas, products, or merchandise

- Be larger than life

- Inspire audience participation

- Create a signature style

- Develop a stage persona

- Manage their own and the audience's energy

- Learn lyrics/lines

- Create an unforgettable experience

- Prepare for Showtime

- Perform a post-show analysis

Continue with This Book If:

- You'd like to apply a framework that will make public speaking a pleasure rather than a pain, giving you the tools to write and deliver a well rounded, satisfying presentation.

- You want to energise your speaking and give your talk all the thrills and excitement of a pop concert from your favourite performer (even if you talk about something complicated like tax or law).

- You want to be guided through the speech-writing process and given step-by-step instructions on what to do before, during and after your presentation.

Maybe you'll never sing live at London's Wembley Stadium. Nevertheless, there's no reason why you can't receive glowing praise for a work talk, or move people to buy your products (merchandise) after you've promoted your business at an event (gig).

What Makes This Book Different?

Over the years I have read many public speaking books written by speaker coaches and voice experts; by business people and actors.

There weren't any books written by singers—books that showed how to be a DIVA speaker and have a good time in the process. Books about how to learn from your favourite pop stars—people who are more accessible (at least via gigs and YouTube) and who you're far more likely to know about than professional speakers who are often only known within their niche or in the worlds of politics, business, and public office.

This book will help you develop your own DIVA style, whether you're a Beyoncé, an Adele, a Taylor, or a Gaga. These singers are all world-class mega stars and each in their own unique way. It's time to learn how to be a uniquely fabulous speaker and excel at being YOU on stage, playing to your strengths and building on your weaker areas to create a rich and valuable experience for your audience.

The book also deals with your mindset and takes you through everything you need to consider on your presentation journey. As you read, keep in mind your favourite gigs, your favourite performers and start figuring out what your DIVA persona is. We'll translate that into your speaker persona and all that comes with it. By the end of this book, I hope you'll be raring to perform on stage and give your next speech!

Who Should Read This Book?

- Perhaps you're an entrepreneur and want to grow your business.

- Or maybe you need to speak to your community?

- You speak to groups at work during meetings or presentations.

- Or perhaps you would like to have more influence and be seen as a leader within your group or organisation.

- You know you need to communicate more powerfully and are figuring out how to do just that.

- Do you like having attention focused on you?

- Do you enjoy expressing yourself with words and actions?

- Do you have something to say and would like to channel your inner DIVA to get that message across in an exciting way?

- Have you already tried public speaking and want to improve?

- Are you frustrated that you're unable to get your point across with impact and energy?

- Is there a bigger and more exciting you, waiting to emerge from the wings?

If you identify with any of these scenarios, then this book is for you.

Whether you run a business and want to get out and speak to drum up more leads and customers, or for personal reasons, *you just know* it's time for you to be seen and heard, there are tools and tips here for you.

There's no reason to bore your audience. Just because you've seen many dull speakers, you don't have to be one too. Make people feel they've had a great experience and they're more likely to want to get to know you and do business with you. You'll be seen as a leader and will have more influence over those around you.

One of the unique aspects of this book is the DIVA Speaking System™. It's not unique to have a system. You may have heard of 'The 6 Cs' or 'The 3 Ts' or something similar.

I created the DIVA Speaking System™ as an easy way to remember all the main skill areas that are required to be a well-rounded and effective speaker.

But first, let me tell you my own story of how I went from timid introvert to professional singer and award-winning speaker.

My Story

"I'm sorry Shola. You're fired."

I don't think I'll ever forget those words, delivered in my boss's broad Yorkshire accent.

What? M-m-m-me? Fired? H-h-h-how?

As a young girl, I'd always worked hard and been a good girl, if a bit geeky. I'd studied the sciences, and had been happy to lurk in the background. I kept a low profile, while producing solid—if uninspiring—results that got me into university, through the process of becoming a qualified teacher and then into a master's degree programme. Eventually, I ended up working in the USA as an IT/management consultant. Returning to London, to the role of Account Director at a small print and design agency, I'd been required to manage meetings with senior board-level clients; to take the reins and run with them and speak persuasively in front of groups.

It was here that I discovered that I was scared. I was scared to speak up. Scared to express myself. So frozen and afraid of being seen by my peers and bosses that my mind turned to mush. It was horrible and debilitating.

Over time, I developed a three-part strategy to try to get away with my lack of contribution and general uselessness during meetings. Firstly, I would scribble down plenty of notes – it made me look busy. Secondly, I'd smile—no, grin—at everyone who spoke, hoping it was enough to be likeable and enthusiastic. Thirdly, I would nod my head so vigorously that once or twice I developed a migraine. Seriously.

I thought I'd got away with it. I was wrong.

Eventually, my client complained to senior management that his account director—err, yes, me—was not doing a good enough job to warrant the fee they were paying for my services.

So, I was out.

There I was, having to move out of the smart Central London flat I'd been sharing, and in with my little sister. A year before that, I'd been living the life in a brownstone apartment in Manhattan's Greenwich Village, daily retracing the steps of Carrie and the other fabulous ladies from the TV show 'Sex and the City.'

How things had changed. Now, I slept in a single bed in my sister's small spare bedroom while I contemplated my next career move and wondered what had gone wrong. For a while, the only steps I retraced were the ones to the local job centre.

Looking back at that time, I'm grateful for it. Firstly, because it made me realise that I was in the wrong career and secondly, because it was during my spell out of work that I finally decided to take the singing lessons I'd dreamed of since I was a young girl.

After a while, I trained to be a life coach and that gave me the courage to embark upon a career as a singer. A slightly introverted singer, but a singer nonetheless. Over the years, I learned—sometimes the hard way—to be in front of audiences numbering from a handful to thousands. I also discovered how to write catchy words in the form of song lyrics, and to engage people in my shows.

Eventually, I had to tackle my fear of public speaking.

I was reading Brendon Burchard's *The Millionaire Messenger* and had reached the chapter on becoming a personal development trainer and speaker. I was in for a big surprise!

While I was reading the chapter, I felt tears well up in my eyes and I started crying.

But these weren't tears of sadness. More like tears of excitement, hope, and anticipation! Something deep within me stirred, and a part of me I didn't realise existed effectively sat up, and said, "Listen to me!"

I wasn't quite sure where being a speaker would take me. I didn't even know what I wanted to speak about! But I felt I owed it to myself to explore and honour those emotions. To cut a long story short, I eventually listened to that voice and, two years later, I joined Toastmasters, the worldwide public speaking and leadership organisation.

To my surprise, I found that I LOVED public speaking. Soon I was being paid to speak. I won a couple of awards. Thankfully, I realised that to be a decent speaker you don't need 'the gift of the gab' nor to be slick and fast spoken. With good intentions and the audience's interests at heart, it is possible to create and deliver a message that can entertain, inspire, and transform.

And then, in a single week, at a public speaking club, I heard three women—all kick-ass, successful women—saying that if they could have been in their dream career, they'd much rather have been a singer.

What?

These people had already enjoyed plenty of public speaking opportunities and yet still wanted to sing? I figured that if I could explain how similar speaking and singing actually were, there would be a number of results:

1. We would realise what a great privilege it is to speak in public.

2. We would enjoy the public speaking experience so much more and treat it as an exciting way to make a connection with our audience.

3. We would take the opportunity to channel our inner DIVA and have a delicious time on stage instead of allowing fear to take over.

So, my own public speaking programme, Speak Up Like A DIVA (www.sholakaye.com), was born. I now train people to be better presenters at my London-based public speaking club, online, and in the corporate world.

Read on if you'd like to release your public speaking DIVA, enjoy the enormous privilege of speaking to audiences and deliver huge value on stage.

Chapter By Chapter

You can either read the entire book from cover to cover, or jump to the parts you're most interested in.

Do you feel your speeches lack excitement and energy? Then start with Chapters 2 and 3 on how to be **DYNAMIC**. If you're just starting out, it might be an effort to incorporate more than a handful of the tips in these sections. That's fine. As you master each tip or technique, plan to add more to your arsenal and you'll become stronger and more confident over time.

If you struggle to involve your audience and want to create a deeper connection with them, go to Chapter 4, be **INSPIRING**. This will teach you about storytelling and inclusive language that engages your audience.

Want to find out how to structure your content so you can provide your audience with lasting value? Then go to Chapters 5 and 6 that show you how to be **VALUABLE**.

If you feel you're a bit of a fake on stage, or you're not sure 'who you are' when you're up to speak, start with Chapter 7, and uncover your **AUTHENTIC** self.

The latter part of the book, from Chapter 8 onwards, "Writing Your Speech", "Finding Speaking Gigs", "Preparing For Showtime", and "Showtime and Beyond" are about the nuts and bolts of writing and delivering your speech.

If you're planning a presentation, I definitely suggest you read these latter chapters, as they will provide you with the many fundamentals of speechwriting and stagecraft. You can then supplement this information with some of the tools and tips from the DIVA Speaking System™ detailed in Part 1.

At the end of each chapter is a **DIVA CHALLENGE.** These tasks will move you forward on your speaking journey and will help you consolidate what you've just learned. A workbook containing these challenges and other exercises can be found at www.sholakaye.com/divabookcourse.

So, DIVA, I hope you enjoy this book and get real benefit from it. Get ready to sing your song, speak your words, and be your magnificent, fabulous self!

For The Men Reading This

Fellas, this book is not intended to alienate you and you can still benefit from the DIVA system, described in chapters 1 – 7, and all the chapters in the second half of the book on crafting and delivering a speech.

I did think about presenting the system for both genders and using the terms DIVA/DIVO, where DIVO is the male counterpart. Eventually, I decided against it.

There are plenty of public speaking books out there and many of them quote from the great male public speakers without giving women much of a look in. In this book, the majority of examples I use are of women performers or indeed from my own experiences on stage, as both a singer and a speaker. It doesn't mean that men can't learn from those examples too.

So guys, when you see the word DIVA, look at it as just that. A word. It doesn't exclude you because it's in the feminine. Break the word down into its constituent letters, D-I-V-A, apply the system, and prepare to rock the stage!

***

So reader, what's *your* DIVA style? In the next chapter, we look at the DIVA Speaking System™ in more depth and explore how we can use the examples of pop divas to help us become better speakers!

Part One

Chapter 1
The DIVA Speaking System™

Have you ever been to a show or watched a performance and felt there was something missing? Perhaps the performance was wooden, or it didn't touch your heart—there was no connection or excitement. Maybe you thought the speaker was going through the motions or their voice was dull and lifeless. Or they came across as fake or uncomfortable.

There are many moving parts to a good performance. You need to achieve the balance between being uniquely you and including crowd-pleasing aspects to make sure your audience has an enjoyable and valuable time. The DIVA system will help you create a well-rounded, entertaining presentation that allows you to be yourself while keeping the audience satisfied, too.

The DIVA Speaking System™:

D – Dynamic – Be vibrant and energetic

I – Inspiring – Evoke a powerful emotional response

V – Valuable – Know your stuff—it's all about the audience

A – Authentic – Be yourself

Think of each part of the system as one of the legs of a chair; perhaps a red, velvet chair with a luxurious furry cushion sitting on top! The kind of chair you might find in a DIVA's dressing room. Before you speak, think about sitting on that chair, and all four legs being solid and supportive. Don't consider going on stage without your seat being sturdy (as well as gorgeous and inviting). If you do, you may well find that your performance is less DIVA, more dull and dreary.

The DIVA system can sit alongside any framework you use to arrange your content because it's about who you're being and takes a holistic approach to your worth as a speaker.

For each of the four areas of the DIVA system, I've assigned some singers I feel would help explain the concept. Apologies if I've left out your favourite singer. I've chosen entertainers that almost everyone will have heard of, including a few who were very famous a while back and not as 'of the moment' as they once were. Hopefully, you'll still recognise them.

Dynamic – Lady Gaga, Pink, Madonna

These performers are quirky and energetic. Their goal is to put on a great show, all the while being creative and sometimes a little bit edgy. From Pink trapezing above her audience during her live show, to Lady Gaga dressing up as a piece of steak, there's never a dull moment with these entertainers.

Perhaps you're the same. It's important for you to create a unique experience for your audience. You're fired up by the thought of designing some exciting slides. You love to use the stage as your playground. You hate the idea of being trapped behind a lectern and love the prospect of dramatic hand gestures, audience interaction, lots of vocal variety, and a gripping open and close to your presentation.

Inspiring – Taylor Swift, Ellie Goulding, Alicia Keys

These singers are natural storytellers. They use their wordsmith's abilities to bring you into their world with moving stories and scenarios.

Are you similar? Do you enjoy drawing people close to you with touching, heartfelt, or exciting stories? Maybe from your own experience or from the lives of others? You're a natural at taking your listeners on a journey, showing your thought processes, and having them on the edge of their seats as you move to the conclusion of each anecdote.

Valuable – Beyoncé, Rihanna, Diana Ross

These performers are the all-rounders; the entertainers who consistently put on a show with the audience in mind. It's all about delivering value, whether that's with sparkling stage sets, glittering costumes, or perfectly executed dance routines. The audience comes first and they know there'll be something to feast their eyes on during the show.

How about you? When you speak, is your mind set on delivering a high-quality experience to the audience? Is service your highest mission when it comes to speaking? Audience enjoyment, comprehension, and take-home value are the most important things to you and it's paramount for you to be liked and appreciated by anyone who hears you speak.

Authentic – Adele, Aretha Franklin, Celine Dion

These singers are the balladeers. They use their big voices to create a spellbinding experience for the audience. Intimate moments are important to them and they wear their hearts on their sleeves. There may be less razzle-dazzle in terms of glittering sets and dance routines. They make up for it by connecting with the audience using vocal nuance, emotional delivery, and vulnerability.

Is this you? Is it hugely important for you to connect on a heart level when you speak? Do you feel deeply satisfied by showing your 'true' self? Are authenticity and vulnerability more important to you than coming across as crisp and confident?

The reality is that many performers—and speakers, too—fit into more than one of these groups. Once you've decided which group(s) you most identify with, mull over which area you would like to look at first to take your speaking to the next level. Maybe you want to consolidate who you are and read more tips on your predominant style. Or perhaps you want to become a better-rounded speaker and will turn to the sections that complement your natural ability.

For example, if you identify strongly with the DYNAMIC and VALUABLE groups, read the chapters on being INSPIRING and AUTHENTIC. This will help you become a more balanced speaker. Bear in mind that you have your own personal style and may not want to adopt all the suggestions listed. It's important to be yourself, and you need to be comfortable on stage. It's not about twisting and contorting yourself into what you're not. It's about being the best version of you.

What's In A Name: DIVA?

Most of the people I encounter love the name of my business, Speak Up Like A DIVA. They see it as vibrant, sassy, and unique. However, from time to time I meet resistance around the use of the 'D' word.

"I'd change that name if I were you. Divas are bitchy, difficult, mean . . . Why on earth would you associate yourself with that word?"

To those who share this opinion, I ask them to look up the origins and definition of 'diva'.

A quick look in the Merriam-Webster Dictionary says the following:

1. prima donna

2. a usually glamorous and successful female performer or personality <a fashion diva>; especially: a popular female singer <pop divas>

So yes, 'prima donna' fits with that more negative usage of 'diva' while the second definition ties in nicely with the theme of this book.

But, if we look at the etymology of the word, we see the following:

Italian, Literally, Goddess, From Latin, Feminine of Divus Divine, God

And synonyms of 'diva' include goddess, princess, and queen.

So DIVA originally came from 'divus' which means divine or god-like.

Would you like to be a goddess at public speaking? I know I certainly would! Indeed, although I'm not a religious person, to think that the divine inspires my speaking is very encouraging. In fact, in one of my early Instagram memes, I wrote 'diva: a divine woman with a message for the world'.

So, please don't think that being a DIVA speaker is anything besides a positive experience. I hope this book helps you become a goddess, queen, or princess of public speaking. Or maybe all three! Tap into the energy of your divine self as you speak authentically on stage and connect with your audience on both a human and spiritual level.

Anyone Can Be a DIVA

In this book, I mention several examples of pop stars and famous individuals that fit into the DIVA model. It's important to note that you can find DIVA influencers in all walks of life. In fact, some of the most inspiring speakers are 'ordinary' women who found their voice and spoke up at just the right time.

An example of an inspirational woman is Malala, the teenager who spoke up for the education of girls in Pakistan, and was shot by the Taliban. Against the odds, Malala survived horrible injuries and is the recipient of a Nobel Prize.

Then there's Rosa Parks, the quiet seamstress who overturned years of racial segregation in the USA. She had been working tirelessly to secure voter registration for African Americans and to help those who had been victims of abuses. One night, on her way home from work, she took a stand by refusing to give up her seat on the bus to a white man, thereby breaking existing segregation laws. The rest is history.

In my own life, there was my courageous foster mother. She was an English woman who, several decades ago, raised three brown-skinned foster children during a time when the UK was far less of the melting pot that it is today. She risked rejection and snubs from family and neighbours, and yet was undeterred and showered us with her love and affection. Even at the age of 94, living in a nursing home, nearly blind and walking with a cane, I watched her come to the defence of my sister and me when a male resident, 20 years younger and twice her height, challenged our presence. She constantly showed selfless love and a determination to speak up for what is right.

You don't need to be rich, famous, or glamorous to be a DIVA.

Who are the DIVAs in your own life? These are the 'everyday' women who challenge the status quo and speak their heartfelt truths. Women who choose not to go with the flow, but take risks, often in the support of loved ones or a larger cause. These women do extraordinary things, despite having an 'ordinary' life, and it's important to acknowledge their courage. In doing so, we give ourselves space and freedom to be extraordinary too, whether it's on a bus, in a nursing home, or on the stage.

***

In this chapter we looked at the DIVA Speaking System™ and what makes a DIVA.

DIVA CHALLENGE: What's your predominant speaking style?

- Dynamic – energetic, quirky, creative, lively

- Inspiring – earnest, seek to connect, tell lots of stories

- Valuable – put the audience first, want to give them a 'good show'

- Authentic – show your true self, wear your heart on your sleeve.

So, it's time to take an in-depth look at the DIVA Speaking System™. Read the next chapter if you're interested in what makes a DYNAMIC speaker or, jump to one of the later chapters if you feel you have this covered. And get ready to be extraordinary!

Chapter 2
BE DYNAMIC – The Energy & the Audience

Some artists and speakers are natural performers. They live for drama and give their audience a high-energy experience using techniques they've either learned or have somehow known since birth. Maybe they're a little quirky and eccentric, or perhaps they know how to play to a crowd. Think of Lady Gaga when she first burst onto the scene, arriving at the Grammy's in an egg, or wearing her meat dress!

To be a dynamic speaker, it will serve you well to tap into this sense of drama, fun, and creativity. You don't have to wear a crazy outfit or smear yourself with fake blood to add some excitement. Even the most serious work presentation could benefit from some vocal variety or change of pace in the delivery.

Did you ever read a story to a young child? It was probably a great pleasure for you to speak in a dramatic whisper, or imitate the mooing of cows and the neighing of horses to bring the story to life. Or maybe you were enjoying a game of hide and seek, running here and there, and playing full out in a fun and uninhibited way.

Learn to be dynamic in your own style. As you read through the various suggestions, think about who you are and how you'd like to come across on stage. Quiet and competent? Vibrant and vivacious? Loud and lively? Informative and intense?

Read on and learn how to play with the energy like a superstar.

The Audience Wants You to Do Well

Have you ever had nightmares about the audience? Did they devour you with their eyes? Chew you up and spit you out? Did you imagine them hating you and wanting you to do badly? Near the end of the nightmare, did they descend on you like a pack of wolves, or chase you down like the zombies in MJ's Thriller video?

If so, stop! Wake up now! I want to share a secret with you. Are you ready?

The audience wants you to do well. Yes, you heard correctly. They WANT you to do well. They're willing you to do a great job and ensure their time with you is well spent. Even the people who sit in the audience and seemingly glare at you with a stony face, want a decent show.

I can't count the number of times where I've been singing or speaking, and there's been someone in the audience who's poker-faced throughout. They don't smile at my jokes. They don't nod during any of the questions. They just seem to glare at me intensely the whole time.

And yet, when the show is over, those are often the people waiting in line to tell me how much they enjoyed it.

Never judge a book by its cover. Maybe they are so gripped by you that they've temporarily forgotten how to smile. Maybe they suffer from resting bitch face! Give them the benefit of the doubt and assume they are fascinated and entranced by your incredible performance.

Not everyone will love you, of course. People have their preferences. If it makes it easier, think to yourself that a proportion of the audience will absolutely love you—especially if you invite your entire family, everyone from your yoga class, and your best friends.

Then there will be those that hate you. Maybe they don't like your hairstyle or the way you speak. Perhaps someone dragged them along and they hate the topic. You can't do anything about this, so just ignore it.

The majority will be indifferent. These are the people you want to win over. They're open to influence; they are curious and want a good show. Work on getting these guys to love you by offering them a DIVA presentation and you can go to bed and have sweet dreams without a zombie in sight.

Get the Audience Involved

Did you ever go to a gig where the performer didn't interact with the audience at all? All night long, you waited for that moment where the star would talk to you and the rest of the crowd, and make you feel special, but it never happened.

Even a quick "Hey [Birmingham], how you doin'?" [Insert your location as appropriate] would have satisfied you. Yet you got . . . nothing. The audience might just as well have not even been there.

Well, the equivalent of that in the world of speaking is *not getting your audience involved and interacting with you.*

What a wasted opportunity, for a number of reasons:

1. Audience involvement raises the energy in the room

2. It takes the spotlight off you, which is great if you're feeling a bit nervous

3. It gives you feedback on how engaged the audience is. If they seem reluctant to participate, then maybe you need to change up what you're doing or create an energiser moment to lift the room and help those who are flagging a little.

One rule of thumb is that you should be injecting some kind of audience participation piece every 6 – 10 minutes, depending on the length of your workshop or presentation.

So how do I propose you 'get the audience involved'?

Some easy ways are:

- Hands up participation – Ask a question or make a demand such as "Put your hand up if you've been to France!" Remember with questions and interaction, always ask the flip side too, so that everyone gets a chance to say yes and take part. So also say "Put your hand up if you've never been to France before". Of course, if your talk is taking place in France, then that's the wrong question.

- Ask the audience to interact with each other. For example, say 'Turn to your partner and tell them, "You've got this!"' This serves to get the audience laughing, smiling, and bonding with each other and creates a "We're in this together" atmosphere.

- If they're an 'up for it' group, seated in rows, you can ask them to stand up and give the person on the left a back rub. And then do the same with the person on the right. This is great as an energiser exercise at longer personal development talks. But, be careful. I've seen this exercise backfire when one person refused to participate and said, "I don't know you, so I'm not going to rub your back—it's too personal". This exercise can create awkwardness. Assess the group first!

- Throw a question out to the audience and ask them to shout out their responses, or ask them to put their hands up while you choose who's going to answer.

- Get them to ask you questions, especially during the Q&A session, and invite questions throughout your talk, if appropriate.

- Run a demonstration using audience members. If you're bold, you can even bring an audience member or two up on stage to take part. Take control and give clear directions. When you need them to sit back down, make it very clear. Once the demo is over and before they leave the stage, ask their names, and tell the audience to give them a round of applause.

One thing to avoid is singling out particular audience members to answer a question. Unless they are a plant and you know they can provide you with a good answer, this can backfire. I attended an event where the speaker pointed to an audience member and asked if there had ever been any mental illness in the family. What a question! Of course, the audience member declined to answer and the speaker was left looking quite embarrassed.

A bit of audience participation can be the difference between people dozing off at the back of the room—or even at the front—and everyone sitting up and paying rapt attention. Don't be afraid; get them involved.

Eye Contact Is Important

Some performers have an amazing skill at making every audience member feel seen and included.

As a speaker there's a real knack to giving the audience the feeling that you're all in it together. Part of that skill involves learning where to look. The bigger the venue, the harder it is to make eye contact with everyone. What's important is to make sure you connect with all the different areas of the room. That way, the people seated in the vicinity of wherever your gaze is directed, actually lock eyes with you, and think you're looking at them.

Other points regarding eye contact include:

- Don't sweep the room like the beam of a lighthouse. This is often difficult to avoid early on in your speaking journey. You may be worried that if you lock eyes with someone, you'll forget your lines and it will throw you off your train of thought. This might well happen once or twice. With time you'll get used to it. Ideally, make an entire point, or at least a sentence, while looking at the same person, before moving on.

- Remember to include the back of the room as well as the front, middle and the extremities, especially if it's a wide room. Imagine talking to someone for an hour and they don't look in your direction once. That would be horrible. So don't let it happen with your audience. One tip I've learned is to use a W pattern when speaking. Start at the front extreme left and make eye contact with an audience member in this section while making your point. Then move to the inner left back, come forward to the middle of the group, then move your eyes to the inner right back of the room, before turning your gaze to the front right section of the audience. Afterwards, repeat the pattern, but in reverse. Each time your eyes rest on an audience member, make sure you stay there for at least two or three seconds before moving on.

Years ago, I would travel regularly to Spain to perform. One time, a promoter was a bit over-optimistic about the crowd he thought he could pull in for an event. In a room that would have easily accommodated 300 people standing, only 18 people showed. Ouch! I didn't take it personally and put on my usual dazzling display (or at least I hoped it was!). However, with only a few people in the room and performing for 90 minutes, we were all struggling with the amount of eye contact I could make.

At the beginning of the show, I made a point of looking at each person in turn for a moment or two, but by the time I'd made the rounds of every single person several times (probably by the end of the second song of the set), people were growing uncomfortable. I could see that as my eyes alighted on them, they shifted around and didn't want to hold my gaze.

The lesson here is that you can sometimes overdo the eye contact. Some people will have a better tolerance for it than others. If you see some people eagerly watching your every move on stage and clearly wanting to connect at that level, then feel free to make more contact with them. On the other hand, if you spot anyone who looks unsettled and breaks eye contact as soon as you connect, spare them the discomfort and look at someone else instead, or just give them a quick glance.

Be Bigger Than Yourself

Are you afraid that you need a huge stage presence to keep your audience engaged?

Most likely you're not speaking at a stadium. Even if you were, what would you need to do differently in comparison to talking to 10 people in an office meeting room?

Well, the difference is how much energy you need to bring to the stage. In general, the bigger the audience, the more energy you need.

That doesn't mean you need to act fake. It just means that for a bigger audience, your gestures need to be a little larger, the arms more outstretched, the voice a little stronger (even if you have amplification). It's hard to put a finger on it. However, we've all seen people on stage who are using their usual daily gestures and don't seem to have that extra spark that helps capture the audience's imagination.

It can even be in the mind. Visualise your aura, or energy field, reaching out to fill the entire room and touching those at the very back of the audience, even if you can't actually see them. It will give you a more expanded awareness and help your energy to connect with everyone present.

Ramp Up the Energy in Your Open and Close

Have you been to a show where the opening was incredible and where the end was a spectacle, too? High energy, fabulous singing, amazing costumes, dance routines? Great extravaganzas start with a bang. They also have a finale that keeps the audience marveling and talking, long after the show is over.

Make Your Opening and Ending Memorable

People remember how you open and how you close.

Make sure the energy is high during your opening, and that you also have something impactful to say in closing. Most speakers understand that the beginning is important and they naturally start with more energy. Their adrenaline is pumping, and perhaps they're a little nervous and excited, and that combines to create a natural high-energy opening.

The middle – well, strive to do a good job, but people will forgive you if the energy dips a little here. In fact, it's expected. People can't usually maintain the same high level of concentration throughout your talk. Their minds will most likely wander a little bit, which is why you need to draw them back in towards the end. The mid-speech slump is one of the reasons why it's important to summarise your main points at the end of your talk. I'll cover more of this in Chapters 5 and 6 on being VALUABLE.

At the end of the talk, some speakers trail off. The energy slips away until they give an apologetic shrug of the shoulders that means "That's it, I'm done".

Don't let this be the way you end your speech.

Close your speech with a summary and think up an energetic conclusion. It could be a thought-provoking question or a rousing call to action. Even if your talk has been hard hitting, leave people with hope for the future. If you've delivered bad news, leave people on a positive note. Ask: "What can we do to make this better?" or something else that's inspiring.

Whatever you do, don't be a damp squib and send your audience home on a weak, low note.

Play With the Energy

Exceptional speakers command the attention and emotions of the audience using energy shifts.

What do I mean by that?

Well, you might go to a show and the artist sings a medley of up-tempo pop. The crowd is clapping, dancing and in the mood. Then . . . the lights dim, the artist stops or slows down, and the next song is a touching ballad. The mood of the entire venue changes completely from "Let's go to the club and party" to "Ouch, love hurts". Right here, the artist forges an unforgettable moment for the audience.

Now, a singer has the resources—backing music, staging, dancing and lighting—to help them make that transition. A speaker has none of these tools. However, it's still possible to shift energy. It usually involves a sudden transition from light-hearted to serious, or the other way around. Or from fast-paced words to a long pause, followed by a slower pace with a different sentiment and tone of voice.

For example:

- You're on a roll with your audience, asking questions and having them respond. You're smiling, maybe even laughing at some of the answers. Then, you stop abruptly. You slowly wipe the smile off your face and share a serious or shocking statistic. The energy in the room shifts instantly.

- You're telling them a serious story—your body is still, your motions are full of intensity, they're waiting for a powerful and thought-provoking end to your anecdote, but then you laugh and say, "I don't know what that means but I thought I'd share with you anyway!" The energy shifts from heavy to light and the audience laughs at the release of pressure.

- You're knee-deep in content, explaining how they can implement your tips and techniques to achieve their goals. You then stop dead. Pause, lower your voice, and slowly say, "How would YOUR life be better if you used only ONE of these tools?" You pause again as the question sinks in and the audience takes a moment to think about the future.

Other ways to play with energy include changing up the activities during your presentation. Every few minutes, punctuate your talk with a question to the audience, a physical activity, or have them participate in interactive energising exercises, as described earlier in this chapter.

***

In this chapter, we looked at your relationship with the audience and at how you can involve them in your delivery to forge connections. We also looked at your energy and how you can play with it to create a rich experience for everyone present.

DIVA CHALLENGE: Which of the following areas do you need to work on, or include more of?

- Audience involvement

- Eye contact

- Energetic delivery

- Memorable open and close

- Energy shifts

In the next chapter, we look at more ways to be a DYNAMIC speaker, this time using your words, your body, and the stage. You'll learn some techniques that will help you work the audience like a real professional, so read on!

Chapter 3
BE DYNAMIC – Your Words & Movement

In this chapter, we explore more ways of creating a dynamic stage persona to ensure an exciting experience for your audience. The words you choose, the movements you make and the way you use your stage area all contribute to the impression you give your audience. Top singers take you on a rollercoaster ride of energy and emotion. From high-energy belters to touching ballads, coupled with staging and lighting—they keep us on the edge of our seats full of wonder and anticipation of what will come next.

As speakers, we don't have the benefit of light shows and music but we do have rhetorical devices, visual aids and more at our disposal, so read on to find out how to up the dynamism in your speaking!

Your Voice Is a Plaything – Enjoy It!

Whitney Houston, Chaka Khan, Christina Aguilera, Adele, Janis Joplin—the list goes on . . . What do all these DIVAs have in common? They're known for their powerhouse voices, vocal agility, and multi-octave ranges.

Wouldn't it be amazing to have a voice like theirs—a voice that's instantly recognisable and that can carry off almost any kind of song?

Well, the next best thing for a speaker is to have a voice that's expressive, easy to listen to and has plenty of variety in terms of pitch, pace and volume.

Don't worry, you don't need to have a set of pipes like one of the singing greats to be able to maximise the potential of your voice during your presentations. An awareness of how and when you can use your voice, and how you can train it to be more flexible, is a great start. So let's explore the topic of vocal variety and how you can use it to breathe life into your talks.

The 5 areas you can work on are:

1. Pitch

2. Pace

3. Volume

4. Timbre/vocal quality

5. Pausing

Consider Your Pitch

The sound can emanate from your gut (tummy), your heart (chest), or your head.

- Speak from your gut when you need to sound authoritative and encourage people to take action.

- Speak from your heart when you need to make a connection with people around you.

- Speak from your head when you're making a joke, imitating a child or being light-hearted.

Consider Your Pace

- Speak slowly when you're delivering bad or sad news or making an important point.

- Speak fast when you need to add excitement or urgency to what you're saying.

Consider Your Volume

- Speak quietly (but always be audible to your entire audience) when you're making an emotional point you want the audience to resonate with.

- Speak loudly to emphasise emotions such as frustration or anger, joy or excitement.

Consider Your Vocal Quality

Some singers are amazing at this. They might sing the same phrase at the same volume and pitch, and yet they somehow add different meaning each time, just by the way they alter their vocal quality.

Have you ever noticed how you can listen to some speakers forever while others are a complete turn-off?

This is often due to the quality of their voices.

A full treatment of this is outside of the scope of this book but here are a few tips.

Ladies sometimes speak at a higher pitch than is natural for them. The easiest way to connect with your natural pitch is to imagine there's a plate of food in front of you that you can't wait to consume. What's your favourite dish? Mine is Pad Thai. Yum.

Anyway, imagine a big, juicy plate of food—or maybe it's your favourite glass of wine or a designer handbag—and say "*Mmm*, that looks good!" in a loud, enthusiastic voice. Most likely that *mmm* sound emanated from your gut and was rich, resonant, and warm.

Try your *mmm* again, and this time listen carefully or record it on your phone or another device. That's the part of your voice you should be speaking from most of the time. *That's the sound that will lend authority and gravitas when you need it, and it will cut through a room to make an impact.*

Repeat this exercise regularly and you'll soon find that your voice moves into a good place where it has plenty of volume, resonance, and impact.

Consider Pausing

Regular pauses offer a range of benefits. It's a good idea to pause:

- If you tend to be a naturally fast speaker. Pauses allow the audience to catch up, so the faster you speak, the more frequently you should pause.

- To allow time for the audience to consider the meaning of a certain point.

- To give yourself time to catch your breath and to gather your thoughts for your next statement.

- Before you make an important point.

- After you've made a big point, to underscore its importance.

- At the end of a section, helping people realise that it's time to move on.

A Quick Word about Intonation

Some women (and men too) use 'up speak' or 'up talk'. This is when your pitch rises at the end of a statement, turning it into a question. The result is that you appear uncertain and lacking in confidence.

Perhaps you intend to give a direction:

'Take the last turning on the left'.

It comes out sounding like:

*'Take the last turning on the **left?**'*

Here's what you can do to break the pattern:

1. Develop an awareness of your habit. As they say, 'awareness is curative'. Start noticing the times that you uptalk and mentally correct yourself.

2. Work on your confidence and sense of certainty so you feel happy making declarations without a fear of being judged, or questioned, on your views.

If your peers and target audience 'up talk' too, then maybe it's not an issue. Be aware that for many, listening to a speaker who is constantly turning statements into a question can be off-putting and disconcerting.

Be Comfortable with Silence

I touched on this earlier. Let's look at it again because it's so important to learn to be comfortable with silence. A colleague once told me "A pause always feels longer to the speaker than it does to the audience".

I promise you, the audience loves a good juicy pause, so give 'em what they came for. If you naturally struggle with pausing, one thing you can do is use a counting system to make sure you pause for a long enough time.

- For a comma in your speech, count silently to 1 in your head

- For a full stop or period, count to 2

- For the end of a section, count to 3.

For a deep and meaningful, "Contemplate this!" kind of pause, you can even count to 4 or 5 to make sure you don't steal your own thunder and cheat the audience out of some drama and impact.

Caroline Goyder, author of the book *Gravitas*, talks about the in-breath being the time to gather thoughts, while the out-breath is the time to speak. Use this as a rule of thumb.

Be comfortable with the silence and use it as a soundless way to add drama and spice to your words. An additional benefit of pausing is that it naturally leads you to add more vocal variety to your speaking. All from doing . . . nothing! So don't forget to use this important tool.

Rhetorical Devices

Ironically, a great way of working on your unique self-expression is to read other people's words. Poetry, prose, speeches, and even song lyrics are useful tools to help us tap into who we are.

The key to interpretation is to separate yourself from the way the other artist expressed it, and find your own voice. Which words are important to you? What does the entire piece mean to you and why did you choose it? Where will you choose to read fast and where will you read slowly? Where should you pause and where should you punctuate with sharper articulation?

All these choices, when made on a regular basis, will begin to inform your own speech writing and delivery. It's not about copying others. It's about seeing what's possible and opening up your mind to develop a unique style with which you're comfortable.

Late poet, singer, author, and activist, Maya Angelou, went through a personal tragedy that caused her to be speechless for several years as a child. During that time, she read and absorbed many classic works written by the likes of Dickens, Shakespeare, and Poe. Years later, when she decided to speak again, the voice that emerged was uniquely her own, and yet informed by the great works she had taken in and digested.

Once you've figured out your unique style you can accentuate your own presentations with features of others that resonate with you. Perhaps you're not going to use flowery, expressive language in the monthly team update. However, you might adopt a long pause, or add a rhetorical device like the rule of three, described below, to lend some drama to an otherwise dry meeting.

Below, I've listed a few of the rhetorical devices you'll often find in speeches, poetry, and prose. It might not be your first thought to include them in your own works. Reconsider, because they can genuinely raise the quality of a talk and provide your audience with a richer experience.

1. Rule of three – Here's an example that shows the power of this rule: "If you express your ideas in the form of a triad, they become more rhythmic, more dramatic, and more memorable".

The 'more rhythmic, more dramatic, and more memorable' forms the triad, adhering to the rule of three. Try to use it in your own speaking. It also gives a feeling of completeness. Two points seem too few, four seem too many. Three points are often just right.

Another example is Coco Chanel's quote, "You can be gorgeous at thirty, charming at forty, and irresistible for the rest of your life". This is the rule of three in action with a witty reference to three different periods in a woman's lifetime.

2. Contrasts – In the book *Lend Me Your Ears* by Max Atkinson and also in Nancy Duarte's *Resonate*, CONTRAST is described as being one of the most powerful devices. It is contrast that gets people jumping to their feet with an ovation during a political speech, and it's contrast that creates memorable moments and sound bites that appear in the press.

For example, Neil Armstrong's "One small step for man, one giant leap for mankind" employs contrast with the talk of the small step vs. the giant leap, and also with man vs. mankind. You can use contrast in rhetoric and also in emotions and energy.

3. **Alliteration** is when we use a series of words that begin with the same letter. Again, it's memorable and satisfying. The most extreme example of this is in tongue twisters: "If Peter Piper picked a peck of pickled pepper" etc. You can use a bit of it in your talk to create an impact, for example: "My story today involves heartbreak, hope, and happiness."

4. **Simile** – You can use similes to compare two examples. Commonly known similes are "as cold as ice" or "they fought like cats and dogs." Feel free to make up your own. They add depth to your language. However, try not to include too many clichés in your presentation.

5. **Metaphors** – A metaphor implies a comparison between two unconnected words. One of the reasons Dr. Martin Luther King Jr. is considered such a powerful speaker is his use of metaphor, using phrases like "Lonely island of poverty" or "Beautiful symphony of brotherhood".

It might be a bit over the top to pepper your 10-minute business networking talk with such poetic language, but to add a powerful metaphor every now and again will likely be much appreciated and respected by your audience.

6. **Anaphora** – This sounds loftier than it really is and it's actually quite easy to incorporate in your speeches if you want to lift the energy and make a powerful impression. In practise, it means to repeat a word, or group of words, at the beginning of a sentence or phrase. It's this device that helped Dr. Martin Luther King Jr.'s *I Have a Dream* speech become so famous.

- *"I have a dream that . . .*

- *I have a dream that . . .*

- *I have a dream that . . ."*

Maybe you won't write a speech that goes down in the history books and is as well remembered as Dr. King's one. However, if you're looking for ways to spice up your presentation, you can certainly do quite well with anaphora.

Imagine you're a graphic designer giving a talk to a group of business owners. You could easily say,

"It's my hope that every small business has access to great design.

It's my hope that high-quality graphics will be easy and inexpensive to source.

It's my hope that beautiful branding will one day be the norm for all".

Not so difficult to do, and it sounds great—vibrant and dramatic. People like repetition in speeches because it gives them a chance to grab hold of what you're saying, so don't hesitate to use anaphora to create an impact.

Ironically, pop songs, often seen as lowbrow, are packed with anaphora. Here's an example from Ike and Tina Turner's *River Deep Mountain High*:

"It gets stronger in every way
It gets deeper let me say
It gets higher day by day"

Pop writers use anaphora because it makes their lyrics easy to remember and to repeat. Next time you give a talk, use this impactful device to give your words a powerful punch.

Move Your Body

Some performers rove the stage like penned-in animals, while others stay stock-still. You can be effective doing either, or a mix of the two. Just bear in mind that your movements need to be in sync with the tone and content of your talk.

If you're a fundraiser speaking about a devastating famine, it probably won't be appropriate to pace around the stage, unless it's to bring a sense of urgency in getting people to donate funds. If you're delivering sad, bad, or desperate news, stand still so your movements don't distract the audience from your message.

If you're speaking about health and fitness, it might be powerful to use your body to mimic before and after situations—perhaps a person who was slouching and feeling sluggish before, who is now invigorated and full of life, standing tall and looking energetic. Feel free to enjoy the motions. Don't overdo it so it becomes a comedy act. Even if it does, humour is entertaining and helps to energise the audience.

Virginia Satir was a highly effective and recognised family therapist. She devised a system to identify behaviour based on various categories of communication. We'll look at these briefly so you have an awareness of the impression you're making on your audience when you adopt these gestures.

- **The beseecher/placater.** You speak with your arms outstretched and wrists exposed to the audience. Do this when you want the audience to like you or when you want to seem vulnerable and exposed. Too much of this can make you seem a little bit insecure.

- **The leveller.** Your palms are facing down, meaning "I'm in control here—you're in safe hands". Do this when you need people to have confidence in your leadership or direction. Overdone it can make you seem a bit bossy or controlling.

- **The thinker.** Put your hand on your chin and look as though you're deep in thought. Used sparingly, this makes you look like an intellectual with something weighty to ponder. The downside is it can also make you seem distant and disconnected.

- **The accuser.** Point your finger at someone in the audience. Use this very sparingly! It makes you seem angry and looking for someone to blame. If you have to point, use your outstretched hand instead, or point using a fist rather than a finger.

- **The distractor.** Move your hands around excitedly with over the top, restless gestures. Distractors often confuse the audience because their ceaseless hand movements make it difficult for viewers to pay attention to the words. If you know you're guilty of overdoing the gestures, then make a point of speaking with your hands by your sides until you have this bad habit under control. Your natural energy will still come across, even without the frantic gesticulations!

General Advice

Make sure what you're saying is in sync with your body gestures otherwise you'll come across as insincere or inauthentic.

- If you're speaking from the heart and trying to connect, use gestures that show openness and vulnerability.

- If you're trying to instil confidence and convince people you're the right person to lead, then use your gut voice and leveller hand gestures.

- Or if you want to lead, seem earnest and get them to trust you, then use your gut voice with outstretched arms and visible wrists.

Make sure you feel comfortable with any gestures you use on stage, otherwise you might lose your audience rather than win them over. Maybe they won't know exactly what's wrong, but they'll sense something is fake even if they can't quite put their finger on it. Watch out!

If you're trying to connect with the audience, then a combination of the thinker gesture while moving backwards as though in retreat, will probably have the opposite effect. You'll come across as distant and wary.

The best gestures are natural and expressive. If you find yourself over-thinking it then leave your arms by your sides or do what feels natural—with enough practise, you'll eventually find a style that is honest-to-goodness you!

Use the Stage

Have you been to a show where the performer was locked into position behind a mic stand, a piano, or a guitar, and never emerged? Or perhaps you attended a talk where the speaker was stuck behind a lectern the whole time and didn't move.

You can still be an amazing speaker from behind a lectern—think of Michelle Obama or US politician Jennifer Granholm. However, some movement and body language are always to your benefit. It allows you to be more expressive, it helps to wake up your audience, and it generally enriches the experience for you and for them. So if possible, step away from the lectern from time to time, or just go without and own the entire stage!

When you're moving around the stage, bear these guidelines in mind:

1.! Move with purpose. Don't sway from side to side, or shift from one foot to the other. Another no-no is gradually moving backwards while you're speaking. It's a dead-giveaway that you have stage fright. Don't do it!

2.! A basic rule is to start centre stage. Then, if you're talking about a time in the past, move decisively to your right (the audience's left) and make your point. Then as time moves forward, you can move to your left (the audience's right) to make additional points. When you sum up, return to centre stage.

3. You can also block out the stage to be different rooms or places. For example, if you take a trip to the countryside, you can walk to one area of the stage for that particular scene. Remember that once you've used that area for the countryside, the audience will still associate it with just that, so don't go back to the exact same spot and pretend it's your living room!

4. If you do have to use a lectern, then don't stay planted there. Leave your notes at the lectern, take a quick glance at them, and then come out centre stage and make a couple of points. Then subtly move back to your lectern again, glance at the notes, rinse and repeat. If you time it well, the audience won't even notice that you're referring to your notes, or they will think it's perfectly normal. Doing this, you have your notes on stage AND there's the benefit of making a solid connection by removing the obstacle of a lectern between you and your crowd of supporters.

Add Weight to Stay Grounded

When we're very excited and bubbly, our energy can be so light it seems that we're about to fly off the stage! This isn't always appropriate. So here are a couple of tips to help you appear more grounded.

1. Try speaking a little slower. Imagine that your toes are a metronome inside your shoes. As you speak, tap your big toe slowly and rhythmically. If you know you're prone to rushing, this will help you slow down to a reasonable pace. Measured tones imply gravitas and a serious nature.

2. You can also imagine that your pockets are filled with heavy stones, or that you have weighted shoes on your

feet. These techniques will slow you down and help minimise that 'fly-away' feeling.

Wow Them with Visual Aids

Why is it that even the corniest wedding DJ will have a smoke machine, roving lights, and a disco cloth? Because they help to create an atmosphere! These are known as visual aids and they're another way to add some excitement and dynamism to your talk.

Some of the best speakers and storytellers can hook the audience with nothing but their words, gestures, and facial expression. However, the majority of people are visual learners and visual aids are beneficial when you communicate with them. Visual aids can be:

- Props – maybe a toy, a model structure, or an item of clothing. Even something as simple as a water bottle or a post-it note, if it helps convey your meaning.

- Flip charts.

- Slides projected to the audience using slideware such as PowerPoint, Keynote, Google Slides or an equivalent.

More on this in Chapter 8, Writing Your Speech.

Give Them Something to Remember

If you have a special skill—maybe you can do card tricks or you can moonwalk (RIP Michael Jackson)—then try to include it somewhere in your talk. Obviously, only do it if it's appropriate. If you're presenting to your MD in the hopes of a promotion, then it may not be the time to do the splits. But if it makes sense, then go for it!

Whenever I've given a speech and the audience has somehow learned that I also work as a singer, almost without exception, someone has asked me to sing a few words.

It's easy for us to think. "Oh, they won't want to hear/see me do my party trick". You would be surprised. People love novelty and also like to see people do 'their thing', so if it's appropriate, entertaining, and will help to create a unique or valuable experience, then don't hold back. This might well become your calling card and the reason you are chosen to speak.

Even if some of your audience have heard you speak before and already witnessed your party trick, there's always someone who hasn't. Include it again. The majority will enjoy your special skill and will be happy to watch a repeat performance.

What's your party trick? Can you:

- Dance

- Sing

- Whistle

- Do magic tricks

- Do long division in your head?

Whatever it is, if you have one, it can be your secret weapon. Prepare and, when appropriate, use it to give your audience an experience they'll never forget.

Are You a Comedian?

People love humour and it tends to be a quick way to ignite and unite an audience. So, if you can bring humour into your speech, great.

Humour is often waiting to pop out in our talks. We might reveal it with:

- A well-timed pause after we've said something potentially humorous

- Pulling a face or using some ironic body language at the right moment

- Using dialogue. This brings a sense of immediacy and is often funnier than narrating events.

It's hard to teach people to be funny. I'd be queuing up for the lessons with everyone else! A very useful book is Sally Holloway's *The Serious Guide To Joke Writing: How to say something funny about anything*. It really does have some beneficial exercises to help you uncover your inner comedian.

Good luck.

Remember that humour can sometimes cause offence, so be sure your jokes don't create a scapegoat or alienate anyone in the audience. As a rule of thumb, the best person to make jokes about is yourself.

Also, humour travels up, not down. While it's acceptable to make a joke about your thick-skinned boss (you can even check with her beforehand to make sure she's OK with it), never joke about the catering staff or the receptionists who look after you.

***

In this chapter, we explored ways to create a dynamic presentation using your voice, your words, your body and visual aids. If you ever feel your speeches are a bit dull and need some speaker 'spice', this is a good place to start.

DIVA CHALLENGE: Does your vocal variety need attention? If so, which of these areas will you explore first?

- Pitch

- Pace

- Volume

- Pausing

In the next chapter, we look at ways to inspire and involve your audience. If your talks tend to be a bit dry or lifeless, the coming chapter may hold the key to transforming the quality of your presentations!

Chapter 4
BE INSPIRING – Tell Them a Story

Amy Cuddy is a Ted Talk sensation and a Harvard professor (www.sholakaye.com/cuddy). I watched her speak in London. During the entire presentation she stayed fixed in one place, standing beside a huge screen (the talk took place in a cinema). She presented the results of academic research and could easily have come across as dull and dry. However, she discussed her work with sincerity; her slides were vivid and easy to read, and she emphasised her findings with touching stories. The result: a standing ovation.

Storytelling and vulnerability really are secret weapons. Our brains are hardwired to be captivated by stories and we warm to those who are open and unafraid to show their human side. Why not use this knowledge to quickly and easily connect with your audience?

Once a month, I run Speak Up Like A DIVA nights in Central London (www.sholakaye.com). Women come together to network, practise public speaking and listen to a guest speaker from the world of personal development or entrepreneurism. What I've noticed is that whenever the ladies tell personal stories and show their vulnerability, there is so much more connection, networking, and making of new friends by the end of the evening.

This section is about the stories you tell and it provides you with storytelling techniques to draw in your audience and make an impact. Whether you're an accountant, a consultant, or a health practitioner, there is always a tale to be told. Take the facts, weave them into a human interest story and watch the effect it has on your audience. Allow people to buy into you and your presentation by adding drama, vulnerability and personal detail.

In this chapter, I give you several different frameworks you can use for storytelling and connecting with your audience on a human level. Remember we're all human first and job function second, so always seek to connect on a personal level.

Get Them Involved with YOU Focused Language

There is such an easy way to bring people into your speech and create a feeling of solidarity. Unfortunately, it's overlooked by many. Do you want to know how?

Use 'YOU' focused language.

What does that mean? Well, I could start my talk with:

"I'm a photographer who loves taking photos of my children. When I take pictures I use a very cool phone app for edits and it gives me great results!"

OK. You've shared what you do, and that you adore your kids. But it's all about you. How about changing it to:

"Do you have a mobile phone? These days it's so easy to take photos of family, isn't it? Put your hand up if you've ever tried this cool phone app to edit your photos?"

This time, you've included your audience. The words are far more engaging and nearly everyone has a mobile phone. Even if they don't have kids, they've still been included in the conversation. You-focused language might be a little bit more long-winded than a straightforward "Me or I" statement. The benefit is that you bring the audience along with you every step of the way.

Imagine you and your audience are in the room together at the start of your talk. Every time you use an 'I' statement, you walk a few paces ahead of them. Eventually, if you use all 'I' statements, you've left the room, maybe even the building, the town and the country and the audience can't see you anymore. You've left them behind. Maybe they're impressed at how far you managed to go, but they aren't with you. You've lost the connection.

Instead, try using plenty of 'you' and 'we' statements in your talk. Every time you do, you allow the audience to catch up to you. It's like reaching out a hand to them and pulling them forward (or inviting them to move forward) on your journey with you. By the end of the story, you've gone on that journey together. You and the audience are shoulder to shoulder, and you've become a team.

So if you want to inspire your audience, involve them at this level. Without YOU-focused language, you might still get an ovation, but you probably won't cause any lasting impact or change. Use 'you' and 'we' language to include and inspire.

Whet Their Appetites

Imagine a gig where the band plays a few bars of a hit song, and then falls silent. The audience go crazy! They're about to hear their favourite song and they start roaring and screaming in anticipation.

As a speaker, you can do a similar thing and tease people into wanting more. How?

By asking questions.

Don't launch straight into your story. Instead, preface it with a few leading questions.

For example, ask "Were you ever in a situation where you were completely out of your depth?" before you tell a story about being fired from your job. (You can read My Story in the Introduction of this book if you want to learn more!)

Or ask, "Did you ever say something to a family member that caused a huge argument that went on for years?" before you tell a story about a family crisis.

Or build anticipation with, "What's the quickest route to success?" before you give your top ten career tips.

With the right question, expressed in the YOU form, you'll whet their appetite for more. They'll be curious about what's coming next and open and receptive to hearing your full story. Omit this inclusive step and you may be missing out on a huge opportunity to create audience interest.

Be Vulnerable - Personal Stories Have Power

One question I'm asked often is "How appropriate is it to tell a personal story in a business setting?" And my answer is that it's always appropriate. Obviously, the story needs to be chosen with care, but people love a good story.

Particularly powerful are stories where the main character (you or someone else) is seen to be learning something new.

It's a known fact that people don't want to do business with you until they *know, like and trust* you. These relationships can take years to build. Telling a story that shows your vulnerability is a shortcut.

You're helping people get to know you. By sharing information that goes a little deeper beneath the surface, you're making it easier for them to like you. And from the law of reciprocity, if you trust them (with your story), then they're more likely to trust you back.

> **Years ago, I used to play guitar and sing my original songs at open mic nights around London. I was a lousy guitarist. It was actually quite embarrassing for me to play in front of some of the other performers. There were rock goddesses and gods, talented slide guitarists, folk heroes, and loop station experts. Then there was me with my basic palette of maybe 6 or 7 different guitar chords, primary school level strumming, and occasional out-of-tune playing.**

So what I did to distract people from the terrible guitar work was tell stories. Before every song I'd share the story behind it.

And I found that no one cared about my rubbish guitar playing. What they cared about were the stories. People would shout out "Me too!" Some would laugh or yell out "What happened next?"

At the end of the gig, there'd always be a small queue of people keen to speak to me and tell me they'd been in a similar situation. My stories weren't special or unusual. However, I'd had the guts to share them; to make myself look a bit pathetic, or embarrassing, or desperate. I took a risk. The result: people connected with me on a human level.

Soon, I realised that I didn't have to be an ace guitarist or even just an average one. I only had to be honest, vulnerable, and open.

So I encourage you to be vulnerable. Be appropriate for the situation, but if you had a business that failed and you learned something, then share. People will see you as resilient.

If you overcame a crummy childhood to build a successful company, share. People will see you as determined.

If you once got sacked for having performance anxiety during meetings and then became a public speaker, share. People will see you as courageous.

Most importantly, they'll see themselves in you and you'll be building that *know, like and trust* factor.

What if you feel you can't share a personal story?

If you can't tell a relevant personal story, then tell a business story. Talk about a client you've helped. Or even use a parable or folk story that demonstrates your point.

Note this word of caution. Make sure your story is relevant. Don't chuck in a tale of how your pet cat died as a child and you never recovered if it's completely unrelated. If you do this, people will see you as a time-waster.

Always be thinking *what's the point of telling this story? Does it contribute to the outcome I'm looking for?* If the answer is no, or you're not sure, leave it out.

Paint a Picture

When you're storytelling, remember that people need a bit of information about the characters and the setting. But not too much.

If you think about the lyrics of your favourite pop song, the descriptions are very economical, but enough for you to picture the lead characters in your mind.

Don't spend ages creating a flowery scene with lots of description like a Jane Austen novel. The audience shouldn't have to wait too long for you to get into the action. Instead, for each character or setting, provide the audience with just one or two descriptive points. The key is to leave some of it to the imagination. As a result, the audience will create their own pictures. They'll fill in the gaps and will feel closer to the characters.

For example, "She looked like a taller version of Oprah Winfrey" or, "A huge white couch filled the tiny room".

Don't feel constrained to paint your picture using only visual descriptions. You can also talk about what you heard, felt, or even smelled. This is called the VAK system, and yes, you *can* describe smells!

- Visual

- Auditory

- Kinaesthetic (feeling)

- Olfactory (smell)

So, remember to give the audience the benefit of a description before you launch into your story. This will help give it life.

Bring It into the Now

Have you noticed that most songs refer to events that happened recently? Occasionally, you'll hear a song that specifies a date, but usually, song lyrics are timeless. Your speeches should be similar.

First, if you can, speak in the present tense. A story is far more immediate if you say, "I walk into the office and he's sitting there watching me", as opposed to "I walked into the office and he was sitting on a chair watching me".

Bring it into the now.

Also, make the story about a recent event. Do this during your set-up. Even if it happened years ago—unless the timing is relevant to your tale—speak as though it was just a few days ago or last week. This brings a sense of recency to the story. Comedians do this all the time. They rarely say "A few years ago", it's usually "Just the other night . . ."

Breathe Life into Your Stories with Conversation

Have you ever watched a speaker who had good stories and yet, for some reason, she came across as a bit dull, or stodgy? Most likely it's because there was no dialogue in the stories.

Conversation helps your speech come alive. Have different characters with different points of view. Relate their words and act out little scenes. It can open up your entire presentation and it also allows for more humour.

Use dialogue wherever you can. It may only be a couple of words here and there, yet the right language, accompanied by a gesture or a change of facial expression, can provide a much-needed lift, adding emphasis and momentum, even to a work presentation.

Storytelling Framework: Drive That CAR

I'm going to give you three storytelling frameworks here, from basic ones you can apply to any story, to the Hero's Journey that you'll frequently find in Hollywood movies. I'll also touch on a couple more in outline form. Between them, you should be able to tell any story.

In Carmine Gallo's book, *Talk Like Ted*, he describes the *Context, Action, Results* formula. It's basic, and yet works really well. I like to call it the CAR framework because it helps me remember the three stages. So let's look at how to drive that CAR.

When I was a kid at school, I always wondered why no one paid much attention to my stories. I thought they were really exciting, but I could never keep people's attention for more than a few seconds. I'd start chatting while the other kids would look bored, change the subject or even just walk away. Let's explore why that happened, by looking at the CAR framework.

Context

This section comes first. You should be asking yourself:

- Where and when did the story take place? Allow yourself to set the scene quickly.

- Who is the main character, the hero?

- What does the hero want and why?

- Who or what is getting in the way (creating conflict)?

It's difficult to have a decent story without conflict. It's the tension between what the hero wants and what stands in the way that draws the audience in and creates interest.

Think of some pop songs:

- Whitney Houston's *I wanna dance with somebody* – She wants to find a lover.

- Sia's *Chandelier* – She's feeling depressed after too much partying.

- Adele's *Someone Like You* – She wants her ex-partner back but can't have him.

So context is very important, while conflict provides interest.

Action

What happens to the hero?

- How is the conflict resolved?

- What takes place?

Result

How does it end?

- What's the lesson the audience should learn? Don't pound this home. You can be subtle here though not cryptic! Make sure people get the point without making it too obvious. Link back to why you told the story in the first place.

The most common problem in storytelling is a lack of context. That's what I was doing wrong as a kid all those years ago. Many people have a tendency to cut the context short so they can tell the story in less time. The end result is a confusing or unsatisfying experience for the listener.

On the other hand, if you love storytelling and are a chatty person, then your own challenge will be editing your tale to make it lean, spare and with just enough detail, but no more.

Storytelling Framework: The Dip

Lisa Nichols, the author, speaker, and personal development guru who appeared in the film *The Secret*, talks about The Dip as a way to connect with and move your audience.

The Dip formula effectively has three points. In **step 1**, you share where you are now, who you are now and your achievements. In **step 2**, you talk about an extremely low point in your career or life. This is called The Dip. In **step 3**, you describe how you moved from that low point to your current position. You describe your ascent to success, what you've had to deal with and who you are now because of the lessons you've learned.

The key to making this formula work is to use lots of emotion so that people truly feel what you felt. It's so important to describe the dark and troubling feelings of the dip. Disappointment, fear, embarrassment, shame—all those emotions and more, are fair game. A detailed description of these feelings provides context for and connection with the audience, so please don't leave it out, even if it feels uncomfortable.

When using The Dip, *never* forget to include **step 3**. You must never dump negativity on an audience without bringing them out to the other side where they can experience feelings of hope and anticipation for the future.

It's also important to share what lessons you learned that helped you climb out of The Dip. The benefit to your audience is that many of them will take the wisdom of your experience and apply it to their own lives.

Storytelling Framework: The Hero's Journey

The Hero's Journey framework is a little more detailed than the CAR framework. It's good for telling longer or more complex stories.

1. Start with a hero. It could be you, or it could be another person. The story will be more immediate if told in the first person. It's your choice.

2. What's the hero doing? What situation is she facing?

3. Escalate the hero's problems. Maybe it was bad before. Now add an event that makes their situation even worse. The hero is suffering and needs a solution. So now we have a hero and we have some conflict.

4. Introduce a guru. The guru could be anyone—a friend, a lover, a business partner, or a random stranger. It could even be information from a book or an inner voice. The guru's job is to give the hero an insight that will help solve the problem.

5. Allow the hero to apply the solution and solve the problem.

6. Finally, the hero shares the solution with the audience, acknowledges the guru, and outlines how the audience can apply the lessons learned to their own lives or situation.

Note that the guru is usually a third party. If you're the main character, don't attempt to take on the role of guru at the same time. You want to paint yourself as an ordinary girl (OK, an ordinary DIVA) who found out some useful information and wants to share it. This way, the audience will more likely identify with you. If you position yourself as the great hero, who solves her own problems, you might distance yourself from the audience and it will block them from receiving the message. Don't put yourself on a pedestal (even though we all know that you're fabulous!).

More Frameworks

A couple of other story frameworks you can use are:

The Timeline Approach – Use This For a Series of Related Events

1. Set the scene and tell the audience when and where the action takes place

2. Describe the past, then present or future events and relate any relevant story

3. Explain why the events and timings are important.

The Problem/Solution Method

1. Introduce the topic

2. Pose the problem

3. Offer the solution or response

4. Continue until you've exhausted your problem/solution combinations. You can also present all the problems in a batch and then provide all of the various solutions.

5.! Wrap up at the end with your recommendations or insights.

***

In this chapter, we explored ways to inspire your audience. Inclusive language, stories, vivid imagery and dialogue all do an excellent job of bringing your speech to life and leaving a lasting impression. Storytelling frameworks such as CAR, The Hero's Journey, and The Dip make your stories more robust, increasing your connection with the audience, and ensuring you frame your content in an inspiring way.

DIVA CHALLENGE: Apply a storytelling framework from this chapter to one of your personal stories.

A speaker can use a variety of techniques to create buzz and excitement, but it's always best to serve up some steak with your sizzle. We'll look at ways to do that in the next two chapters on how to be a VALUABLE speaker.

Chapter 5
BE VALUABLE – What's the Point?

Part three of the DIVA Speaking System™ is about giving your audience VALUE and showing that you're an expert or an authority on your subject.

Imagine a gig where you expected the star to play their old hit songs that you could enjoy and sing along to. Instead, to your dismay, the whole night was full of unknown tracks from the newest album. There were no crowd-pleaser tunes and the evening was a disappointment.

That's the equivalent of not meeting your audience's expectations.

As speakers, we can slip up by not doing the necessary audience research to find out what they want and need. Sometimes you have two audiences to please—both the meeting organiser who books you in the first place and the people who attend your presentation. It's your responsibility to position your material in a way that's useful and interesting to the audience, and also satisfies the person who hired you.

This next section will deal with your content: what to find out before you write your talk, how to structure your information so it's clear and easy to understand, how to ensure the audience remembers your key take-home message, and much more.

A while ago, I went to see Beyoncé perform at London's Wembley Stadium. I can't confess to being a huge fan of Queen B's music. I attended because I wanted to see a big show. And I had no regrets.

There were dramatic, sparkling outfits with shoulder pads, bustles, and all we'd expect from Sasha Fierce. She performed potentially ankle-breaking dance routines in a pool of water and sang a cappella with the crowd. The woman most certainly delivered visual value, even to a non-fan. As I trailed out of the stadium alongside tens of thousands of Beyoncé supporters, I couldn't help feeling impressed and satisfied by what I'd just seen.

So, read on as we learn how to put the audience's needs first and give them an experience full of value.

Do Your Audience Research

Every star knows who their core audience is. Whether it's screaming teens or the mature over-50s crowd, commercial artists cater to their audience and give them what they want. Failure to do this can mean the end of a career. As a Motown singer, I know that my audience will expect to hear songs from that era and not much else. I personally prefer to sing Jazz, however, it would be selfish and ignorant of me to ignore the audience's needs and create an off-piste set list that didn't satisfy. Not to mention that I probably wouldn't get booked again!

Unless you already have in-depth knowledge of the people attending your presentation, you will need to do a bit of audience research beforehand.

Some of the most important questions you should ask the organiser are:

- How many will I be speaking to?

- What is the expected age range?

- What do they have in common?

- Is there an approximate ratio of female to male?

- What are their top 3 needs?

- What is their interest in my subject matter?

- Are there any sensitive topics to avoid?

- How will they be dressed?

- What are their interests?

- Who is the decision maker?

- What does the decision maker want as the outcome for the talk?

- How much do they already know about my topic?

- Which speakers have they had in the past?

- Which ones were well received and why?

- Which previous speakers were poorly received and why?

- What kinds of anecdotes, stories, and examples will go down well?

- Will they be lively? Example, a free bar might mean many are a little drunk.

- Will they be drowsy? (Maybe you're speaking right after lunch)

- Am I expected to create a handout

- Will there be A/V facilities (More on that later)

- Will many of them have English as a second language (if so, maybe use fewer colloquialisms)

Ideally, you would have these questions in an online form. Quickly tailor the questions with what you already know about the event, and then send them off to the organiser. An additional phone conversation is always good. It can highlight considerations that your email questions missed.

You might also:

1. Ask to speak to two or three typical attendees who can give you the inside scoop on the event and the crowd.

2. Do some research of your own on the industry and the company. You could even read some trade magazines.

3. Chat to other speakers who have addressed this audience before to find out if there's anything else you need to know.

On the day, it's important to find out:

*   What is the mood of the audience? Fun, serious, bored, impatient?

*   Are they being forced to listen or are they there of their own volition?

*   Are there outside events that might influence their thoughts and distract them? For example, unusual weather conditions, public transportation problems, issues at the company or in their industry.

If you possibly can, be in the auditorium or meeting room and listen to the speakers that appear on stage before you. Get a sense of the audience's vibe and energy. Take down any useful or funny references from the speakers. You might be able to use them for a callback. This is when a speaker refers to an occurrence that's happened earlier or *calls back* to the words of an earlier speaker. It reveals your spontaneity, makes the audience feel special and is nearly always a good thing to do.

You can even read the local newspaper that day, or scan a local news website to find ideas to drop into your speech. This will earn you huge respect if you find a topic that resonates with the audience.

Big topics are:

- Local news

- Company news

- World or national news

- Business news

- Sports and outside interests

It's also very important to emphasise any factors you have in common with the audience. People like people who are like them. The more you show similarities, the more you build rapport and chemistry. Even go as far as to use their vocabulary. If you go to a place where people speak slowly, then slow down your own rate of speech. If people speak fast, then pick up the pace a little.

What's the Point?

The next question you really should be asking is, WHAT IS THE POINT?

What do you want your audience to DO after they hear you talk? What do you want them to TAKE AWAY from your talk? Why are you there in the first place?

The reason you need to know the point is so that you **stay on track.**

Don't tell cute stories that are funny but irrelevant.

Don't use slides that look impressive but have nothing to do with the mission of your talk.

Keep it lean and mean.

- Do you want to persuade them to purchase your online course?

- Do you need to explain a new concept?

- Do you want to raise money for your charity?

Stay on track to get the results you want. Don't add any content that doesn't contribute to your overall goal.

What Kind of Speech Is It?

There are many different kinds of presentation. Which of the following do you wish to do?

1. Inform or Educate

Your goal is to provide your audience with a body of content that will help them move forward or increase their knowledge.

2. Persuade or Sell

I've grouped these together because persuasion is at the root of sales. It's about getting someone to do something, whether for your good or their own. (Hopefully both!) You might want them to buy a product or to adopt a different mindset.

3. Entertain or Amuse

Humorous or witty speeches fall into this category. You might be an after dinner speaker and your only goal is to get a few laughs, provide some banter and keep people occupied after they've eaten their meal.

4. Inspire or Motivate

These days, motivational speakers tend to get a bad name because the effects of their teachings don't always last. Someone tells a rousing story about their life. The idea is that their tales of adventure or adversity will motivate you to overcome obstacles and reach for success. Nowadays, there's more of a preference for inspirational speakers. Ideally the result is that the audience will be inspired to change their thinking and therefore change their lives.

5. Transform Your Audience

Transformational speakers are the ones who succeed in getting you to act differently and change your behaviour. Transformational speaking aligns very closely with selling and persuading because, after all, the speaker is helping you change your actions. So they've either sold you on an idea or frame of mind that produces different behaviour. Whether that's buying a product or getting up earlier each morning to fit in a run before work, a transformation has taken place if you adopt new behaviour after the talk.

Arranging Your Content

Depending upon the length of time you have to speak, your content should be arranged into 3 – 5 points. Any more than this may be too many. The more points you have, the less likely the audience will remember any of them. Of course, if you are supplying a handout, then that's no problem because the audience can refer to it after the event.

If you are expecting them to take notes, then go slowly enough to give them time to write or, these days, to take out their cameras and snap each of your slides. Alternatively, you could gather their emails and, after the event, send them a copy of the presentation. This approach has the added benefit of building your list!

If you're not the storytelling type, you might want to use the following system. For each of your 3-5 points that form the body of your speech:

1. Introduce the point by asking the audience a question that draws them in.

2. Clarify your point by giving them the facts or details.

3. Explain and elaborate with a case study, example, or anecdote that brings the point to life.

If you enjoy telling stories, feel free to swap points 2 and 3 around:

1. Draw the audience in with questions or other disruptors.

2. Tell a story.

3. Make a point or give some learning material that's illustrated by your story.

If you are using slides, a nice idea is to have a slide that introduces each new section of the talk. Use a full-page photo or image with the section title on it, or format it using the same branding and colouring as the rest of the presentation. Use large typography for the section title, because it will help the audience move on from the earlier point and proceed with you to the new one.

Display Your Signpost

What goes through your head when you're in the audience and a speaker walks up to the stage? Do you sit there full of hope (or doubt) wondering "What am I going to get out of this?"

It probably feels like a magical mystery ride. And not everyone likes mysteries.

That's why you should *signpost* your content early on in your talk.

What Does Signposting Mean?

It means giving the audience a high-level overview of where you're taking them.

For example:

"This afternoon, we're going to review three ways to save money on your mortgage" or

"I'm going to give you my top four tips on how to choose the best wedding venue."

This satisfies the audience in the short term because they now know where you're going. It also increases their anticipation regarding how useful your information will be and how they might apply it to their own situations.

Plus, the more anally retentive listeners will keep score of how many tips you've promised compared to the number you actually deliver. If you promise to give three solutions, make sure you stick to it, otherwise, there WILL be audience members who call you out.

What For and What's Next?

You've decided you'd like your audience to buy your backpacking holiday to Bolivia.

While you're putting the talk together, after each point you make you should ask yourself **"What for?"** and **"What's next?"**

In other words, "Why did I make that point? What am I hoping to achieve with that nugget of information? Is it relevant? Does it make sense? Why is it there?"

This way, you're continually checking in with your purpose.

Once you've answered **"What for?"** it's time for **"What's next?"** This question keeps you on track. Ask yourself, what's the next logical step or piece of info that I should be revealing to my audience? What creates the smoothest and most sensible journey of information?

Make It Catchy – The Throughline

Pop songs are written to be remembered. They are full of hooks. Little catchy earworms designed to stay in your head and be easy to sing back. You might hear a guitar riff or an instrumental line that repeats throughout the track.

The most important hook in a song is the chorus. There will usually be one or two lines that you remember and sing word for word even after you've only listened to the song once.

"Thriller, thriller night!" from Michael Jackson

Or Adele's "You could have had it a-a-all, rolling in the dee-ee-eep."

As a speaker, your presentations will improve massively if you can come up with a 'spoken hook', otherwise known as a 'throughline' or a 'foundational phrase'. Unlike top songwriters who keep rewriting until there are multiple hooks, riffs, and repeatable lines, speakers don't need lots of them. One strong throughline will do; two or more will become confusing. Your throughline ties the speech together. Use it at the right times during your talk and chances are, your audience will leave with it planted firmly in their minds.

Don't underestimate the power of a throughline. Years ago, I wrote a song called "Note to Myself" with, what I hoped at the time, was a catchy little chorus. No, it wasn't a hit, so maybe the chorus wasn't catchy enough! I performed the song once at a music conference in Los Angeles. A year later, at a conference in London, I bumped into another singer who'd been with me in LA. She said, "Hey Shola, I still remember your song. Wasn't it something about writing a 'note to yourself?'"

A good throughline can be as powerful as a musical or lyrical hook. Most audiences have a very hard time remembering what was said during a talk, so helping them to recall even one single point, by including a throughline, is definitely recommended.

The key is to make it simple and repeatable.

Think of it as a political campaign slogan.

"Making America great again"

"Yes we can"

"I have a dream".

The maximum number of words for a throughline is ideally ten. If it can rhyme, even better, but be careful of it sounding too gimmicky.

Depending on the length of your talk, introduce it near the beginning and repeat it at regular, sensible intervals and during your close. Your audience will thank you for giving them something to hang on to and your message will stick with ease.

***

In this chapter we started exploring how to be VALUABLE. By making sure you've researched your audience, having a strong message and signposting your content, you'll engage them with relevant information. Also, by asking yourself "What for?" and "What's next?" you'll stay on track and won't include irrelevant or self-indulgent material.

DIVA CHALLENGE: Create an appropriate throughline for one of your speeches. Make sure it's snappy and catchy. Whereabouts in your speech will you use it?

In the next chapter, we'll delve into how you can provide even more value as a speaker. We'll examine ways to display your content, and how to ensure the audience understands your message. You'll also discover ways to engage them with a strong open and close.

Chapter 6
BE VALUABLE – What's in It for Them?

This second chapter on being VALUABLE will help you display your content powerfully and effectively. You'll also learn how to open and close with strength and purpose and find out how and when to handle questions from the audience.

Plant Your Seeds

'Plant your seeds' refers to the process of 'seeding'. This is a subtle way of feeding the audience snippets of information that enhance your credibility, or otherwise help you to achieve your overall goal.

Let's say you go to see an up and coming artist who doesn't yet have a contract with a major label. During the show, they might say "Wow guys, it's been a busy day today. Earlier on I was in the offices of Universal with my manager, talking about a few things with their A&R department."

By mentioning having a manager, being at Universal and talking to the A&R team, that artist is implying that they're more than one of the many unsigned. It might plant the seed in your mind that they are going places and that you're lucky to be at that intimate gig because next year they might well be playing arenas. You're thinking you should probably buy one of their signed CDs or T-shirts because it might be worth a lot of money one day.

In the same way, you can seed information throughout your talk. Perhaps you might want to drop in a client success story. Or a glowing testimonial. This information will help increase your credibility.

If you're selling a product during your talk, you might like to mention, casually, that you've only got four left, because they're so popular. Drop in that you're in conversation with a large company that wants to distribute the product because it's so effective.

You can seed in a big and obvious way, or you can do it subtly. It depends on your style and what you're hoping to achieve. Either way, plant those seeds throughout your talk. They will help to strengthen your position with the audience. In turn, it will help them to trust you, and to relax, knowing they are in the right place with the right speaker!

Displaying Your Content

Should you use slides and flip charts?

When it comes to visual aids to display content, the common choices pretty much include projected slides or flip charts. You might also have the option of using video.

Flip charts are really handy for capturing and displaying information in real time. As you complete each page of the chart, you can tear it off and stick it on the walls around the room for easy reference. This is very useful during workshops.

Bring along your own markers or ensure that the markers left out for you work well and are easy to read. There's nothing worse than sitting at the back of the room, straining to read the chart when someone has written in a difficult to read colour like red or orange. Likewise, it's frustrating when the ink in the pen is drying out and the writing is faint, or the scribe has untidy handwriting.

Although PowerPoint tends to be the norm during many presentations, there is also slideware such as Google Slides, Keynote for Mac, and many others. There are some wonderful books written on presentations alone, especially Garr Reynolds' *Presentation Zen* and *Slide:ology* by Nancy Duarte, so I won't go into too much detail here.

I'll give you my top three slideware tips:

1. Before you start creating slides in your preferred software, map out your entire presentation using sticky notes.

Use one sticky note for each slide. If your slides are content-heavy, you may not be able to get all the info on each sticky note. At least write down the slide heading or something that will remind you what the content is. Once you have a sticky note for each slide, you can rearrange them at leisure until you're happy with the right order. Only then should you start preparing your slides on the computer.

The advantage of this technique is that it's so much easier to move sticky notes on a table or wall than alter the slide order within your chosen slideware. You can see all your sticky notes at once, and moving them around is quick and easy. Seeing the info summarised on the little pieces of paper can also spur the mind to come up with creative ideas on how to display each point.

2. Use large images in your presentations.

Ideally, use photographs and size them to cover the entire slide. If your presentation is text-rich, use full-page photos as section dividers to give the audience a breather from the text. Appropriate imagery allows the audience to form visual connections with your content, and it looks stylish and modern.

3. Don't read your slides verbatim or turn your back to the audience when you're presenting.

A few weeks ago, I went to see a professional speaker present at a personal development evening. We were in a large lecture theatre and her slides were projected to a huge size. Can you believe that this presenter turned her back to the audience, stood in the middle of the stage area, and read the slides word for word? Her credibility plummeted and I struggled to stay interested in the rest of the talk. What made it worse was that the information on the slides was about the presenter and her family. Surely, she could have spoken about her own life and loved ones without having to refer to a slide?

In PowerPoint, you can use a tool called presenter view. This shows the main slide, the next slide, and your notes. Get to the venue early and set up your laptop or the dedicated computer and make sure it's in presenter mode. Find a place to stand on the stage where you can angle the screen towards you and view it while still facing your audience. This will help you avoid turning your back to read your slides.

Again, try not to read your slides word for word. Ideally, you'll be paraphrasing what's there, adding your own hints, tips, and insights, and elaborating upon the points on the screen.

Word of warning: In some venues, it will be logistically impossible to present with a computer screen facing you, showing your slides while you speak. Ensure that you are familiar with your slides and the order of your presentation or take note cards along as prompts.

Help Them Understand

When you're teaching your audience new content, or perhaps giving them technical or dense information, it's important to break it down so that everyone understands.

Some of the ways you can do this are:

- **Comparisons**. If you come from a small village, maybe the easiest way to give people a sense of its size is to say, "For every one person living in my village there are 500,000 people living in London".

- **Examples**. It's good practise to illustrate information with clear examples. Use names, places, or descriptors that will help visual learners capture the situation in their mind's eye. Contrast: "My client saved 10% on her car price" with "My client, Rebecca, saved £10,000 on the cost of a new red Mercedes." Only a couple of words more have been added and we can paint a clearer picture.

- **Metaphors and Analogies**. Metaphors were mentioned in Chapter 3 on being DYNAMIC. It's worth giving them a second glance here. Aristotle said that to be a good teacher "It is necessary only to be master of the metaphor". This involves using what we already know to help explain the unknown. Look for everyday examples that might be used to explain more complicated concepts or processes. For example, the nucleus of an atom could be described as being similar to a tennis ball inside a stadium.

- **Stories**. A quick story or case study to illustrate your point can work wonders, both for audience understanding and for your own credibility. Again, be descriptive. Don't go too far by cramming your tale with needless detail that suffocates the listener's imagination, rather than stimulating it. Check out Chapter 4 for more on storytelling.

- **Pictures, Photos, and Physical Objects**. As they say, a picture speaks a thousand words. If you have photos to illustrate your point please do include them. Again, make them nice and large, ideally occupying a whole slide. You can bring physical objects such as models or even wear a costume if it helps drive your point home and increases understanding.

- **Questions**. These can be wonderful for encouraging the audience to think. If your content relates to making a decision, you can ask, "What would you do in the same situation?"

Another important consideration is the VAK system. I mentioned this in Chapter 4 on being INSPIRING. Most people process information in one of three different ways. They may be visual, auditory or kinaesthetic. Visual people need to hear expressions like "Do you see what I mean?". Auditory learners are stimulated by language such as "I can hear what you're saying" while kinaesthetic learners are more focused on feelings. For example, "I can feel where you're going with this", or "My gut reaction is to agree". Try to mix up your language so that you touch all three groups.

How Will You Open and Close?

In Chapter 2 we talked about the *energy* of your open and close. The *content* of these two sections of your talk is important too. Remember that your opening can create value for your audience. The right question or quote can frame the entire speech, putting everything you say in context.

Now we take a more in-depth look at your close.

Regarding Your Close

In my years of performing on stage, I always took it as a slight affront if the crowd didn't ask for a couple more songs at the end of my set. During a musical performance, people can let you know if they want an encore by shouting out "One more!" It's not the same when you're making a speech.

In speaking, the audience show their appreciation with a standing ovation or some hearty cheers. Help them out by providing them with an inspiring ending they can appreciate.

Closing your speech is an art. Many people go in with a bang and out with a whimper. Don't spoil a perfectly good speech by ending abruptly and sidling off the stage with an embarrassed look on your face.

In his book *Instant Speaking Success*, the American speaker Paul Evans says, don't close a speech. Instead, 're-open' it.

End your speech on a high and hopeful note. In a way, the end of your speech is just the beginning for the audience.

Imagine you've just run your lap of a relay race and you're now handing over the baton to the members of the audience. You're urging them to take your information, apply it, and execute on the call to action. You're encouraging them to run a race that might even change their lives. Therefore, it could be the start of something big for them. Your close should end with hope, with energy, with an air of possibility, and a sense of "What's next?"

A good way to end is with a recap of what you've covered. You can say "In conclusion" or "As I come to the end of my talk . . ." or something similar. Then précis your content with a summary of your top three points (or fewer depending on how much time you have). You then want to make your call to action.

Earlier in this book, I discussed the idea of having a core message, a throughline or a foundational phrase that summarises the essence of what you want the audience to take away. This is the time to repeat that phrase and also to add any explanation or moral to the story that helps to drive the point home.

You could also:

- Ask a thought-provoking rhetorical question to get the audience thinking about your content and how it applies to their own lives.

- Recite a statistic, perhaps the same one you opened with, and ask the audience what they're going to do about it.

- Tell a powerful story that sums up your message.

Get them thinking and acting, and you've created transformation. This may be something as small as signing up to your mailing list. Once you have their contact details, you can then continue the conversation and help ensure their transformation takes place.

Save your close until AFTER your Q&A. Close with energy and feeling. Remember that this is one of the most memorable parts of your talk.

If you have a trick up your sleeve that you can delay until the end, then it's a great way to go out with a bang. The audience will be buzzing and wanting more, and you'll have lifted the energy in the room.

Answering Questions

As mentioned, it's a good idea to conclude your talk *after* the Q&A rather than before. Q&A sessions can be difficult to control and it's better for you to leave the audience with a positive final image of you and your presentation. You don't want the audience to remember you as the person who became flustered when asked a tough question. Or the one who kept saying "Hmmm, don't know the answer to that. I'll try to find out for you".

That's why I advocate having your Q&A as the penultimate section of your talk.

Near the beginning, during the Signpost section, tell them:

"There'll be a ten minute Q&A section near the end of the presentation and then I'll close it out with a few more words of my own."

That way the audience knows what's coming.

Sometimes, people will ask questions during the talk. If you don't want your flow interrupted, feel free to tell them there'll be a Q&A at the end. If it doesn't bother you to stop and start during your presentation, then take questions throughout the duration of the talk.

When I speak to teens and young people, I want them to have a strong sense that it's a genuinely interactive session and that we're in this together, so I encourage questions throughout.

With adult audiences, if the talk lasts 45 minutes or longer, I also like to field questions as I go along. It lets me know which parts of my presentation the audience finds particularly engaging and it also feels more spontaneous and energetic. Towards the end, I'll have a short Q&A session, too.

Do what feels right for you. Taking questions as you go along can be harder to control. On the flip side, it can make for a more lively presentation. If there are too many questions and you're running out of time, feel free to say, "Sorry guys, I really want to answer all the questions but there's a certain amount of material I need to get through, and I don't want you to miss out."

Another problem that comes up during the Q&A is not knowing the answer to the question. To reduce the risk of this, it's worth taking time beforehand to anticipate the most likely questions that will pop up. Prepare your answers accordingly.

During the talk, if something arises that stumps you, try not to say, "I'll find out and come back to you" as it can give you extra work and can be unsatisfying to the listeners. Instead, throw it out to the audience. Ask them "Does anyone here have the answer to that question?"

Sometimes you will find the same person asking questions again and again. This might be helpful if they're the only responsive person in the audience! If it becomes too much, feel free to say to them "Thanks, I've answered a few of yours already and I'd like to include some questions from others in the audience" or whatever's appropriate.

At the end of the talk, you might encounter people who want to chat to you for ages, monopolising your time. This is a great moment for you to network and make new contacts or business leads. To avoid your time being monopolised and prevent missing out on key opportunities, you can say "I'd love to chat about this further, but I do need to meet the other people waiting right now. Here's my card. Why don't you email me and we can take this further?" Chances are they'll be happy to keep in touch, and now you've freed yourself up to speak with the rest of your adoring new fans!

***

In this chapter you learned about seeding, opening, closing and managing questions.

DIVA CHALLENGE: Think of two or three client stories or examples. Use them to seed your next speech.

Now it's time to look at the final part of the DIVA system: How to be AUTHENTIC. One of the most exciting aspects of public speaking is the opportunity to share ourselves and truly connect. Head to the next chapter to find out how you can give the amazing gift of 'YOU' to your audience!

Chapter 7
BE AUTHENTIC - Show Them Who You Are

This is the section where you add your secret ingredient to the pot. YOU!

My Speak Up Like A DIVA clients often worry about how to maintain their authenticity and sense of self on stage. They want to utilise the tools and techniques at their disposal to become better speakers. What they don't want is to appear artificial or inauthentic.

How can this be achieved?

Nina Burrowes, author of *The Little Book of Authenticity* argues that the word 'authenticity' is related to the word 'author'. Burrowes claims that being authentic is not only about being open and honest. It also means being the author of YOU. Your behaviours, thoughts, actions and values should emanate from within, rather than be forced upon you from the outside.

In this section, we look at values, personality profiles and personas and how they can help us be more authentic by showing us who we are. This idea of being our own authors is so important because as humans, we are not fixed. We can change who we are at any time if we have sufficient impetus and motivation to do so. We've all heard about the long-time smokers who overnight decided they would never smoke again. Provided our WHY is big enough—more on that later—we can change ourselves in whichever way we choose.

So the key here is to decide **who** you 'really' are and **how** you want to come across and to let that shine through. It's about allowing certain aspects of yourself to be more visible.

In this chapter, you're going to be digging deep into who you are, what drives you and motivates you, and what your values are. The better you know yourself, the more you know which parts to emphasise on stage and during your speech writing process. This might affect the stories, anecdotes, and examples you choose to use, the language you adopt, and even how you choose to move and speak.

At the start of your speaking journey—while you're still getting used to your on-stage persona—this process is very important. As you present more and more and find out what works for you, this will become automatic and you'll do it without a second thought.

A few moments ago, I watched Adele on YouTube, singing her huge hit *Someone Like You* at London's Royal Albert Hall. There was no dancing. Adele's feet stayed planted firmly in place the whole time. However, the performance was mesmerising. Her face was expressive and passionate, her hand gestures invited the audience to feel her pain. Her powerful voice filled the theatre, and towards the end of the performance, the audience joined with her to sing the chorus. You can bet that no one there will ever forget the moment they sang alongside the multi-Grammy winning artist.

Adele wore her heart on her sleeve and was authentically herself as she sang. She didn't need to create a sexy dance routine or pace around the stage to get her message across. She was her most authentic self and it was more than enough.

We now explore who YOU are and how to convey that on stage. The audience wants to connect with a real person, not someone who's going through the public speaking motions—using hand gestures or movements that seem robotic and unnatural for their personality.

Read this section to gain insight into what makes you tick and how you can show that to your audience. Learn to create a genuine connection while being your true self.

Who Do You Think You Are?

When I started out as a performer, it was my plan to get as many bookings as possible, fast. To achieve that goal I needed to find a way to stand out from the crowd and offer something a little different. I decided I would perform Motown with a beehive wig and 60s dresses. I quickly found a suitable wig and purchased some 60s outfits. Before long I was being booked and working around the country and even internationally.

For a while it was fine. However, the reality is that I'm not one for dressing up and it's important to me to be who I am, even while performing. Eventually, I grew fed up with having to cram my hair into a wig every time I performed and wearing 60s go-go boots that cramped my toes. To be honest, I'm a comfortable shoes kinda gal.

While I realised that the audience were the main concern, I also felt that wearing clothes that were more 'me' would translate into a better, freer performance. So eventually I found a way to be a Motown singer in my own style.

Similarly, it's important for speakers to be genuine and authentic when they're doing their thing on the stage. That's why I'm including this section on Core Values. Our values are what guide us. Our values steer our lives in a particular direction, knowingly or unknowingly.

My early speeches would typically revolve around a few different topics:

- •! Education and personal growth

- •! Stories about leaving the corporate world and becoming self-employed

- •! Lessons I'd learned in life (often the hard way)

And if I go back even further to my songwriting days, I would often write about similar topics:

- Growth through life experience

- Being independent

- Learning lessons from personal relationships

No surprise then that when I did a Values assessment, three out of my top 10 values were:

1. Freedom

2. Personal growth

3. Education and learning

Those values are the reason I'm self-employed and the reason I love to learn and teach new concepts and ideas.

By looking at our values we can see a clearer picture of who we are, what we hold dear, and how we can incorporate what's important into our everyday lives. It also helps explain some of the conflicts we have, both with other people and within ourselves.

Importantly, knowing our values can help us become more authentic speakers.

What Are Your Values?

By knowing your values you'll be fully aware of your strengths and can use them to become a better speaker. You want to be in your own power on stage. Public speaking may currently be an ordeal for you (hopefully not after you've read this book!) so the idea is to play in your zone of greatness whenever you can.

So, how do you find out your values? There are many websites that host values determination assessments. I recently came across the Barrett Values Centre. There is a quick, interactive assessment on their site that you can try. The Barrett Values Centre will email you your results along with an analysis. (www.sholakaye.com/pva)

There are many similar assessment tools online so do Google around to find one you like.

In effect, you will need to review a list of values and choose your top 10. Once you have done this, think about how they can apply to your public speaking journey.

Mine were:

- Competence

- Continuous learning

- Creativity

- Entrepreneurial

- Fairness

- Health

- Independence

- Integrity

- Personal growth

- Well-being (physical/emotional/mental/spiritual)

Not every value will relate directly to your public speaking journey. However, many will.

For example, when I look at my own list:

- Entrepreneurial relates to the type of people to whom I enjoy speaking

- Creativity explains why I crafted a speaking system

- Fairness comes into play when I deliver my live training. I make sure every attendee has a chance to take centre stage and speak to the group

- Competence will ensure that I always strive to deliver to a high standard

- Continuous learning means that I'm constantly reading, attending training, and trying to find useful advice I can pass on to others.

What about your own list? Which of the items can be included in your speaking?

- If you love creativity, how can you make your talks a little different or quirky so they reflect that value?

- If one of your values is family, perhaps you will include stories and anecdotes about those close to you.

- If it's humour or fun, then you might want to include jokes (if appropriate) or amp up the entertainment with different voices, dialogue, and humorous expressions on your face. You could even show a funny YouTube clip that relates to your material.

By running through this exercise, you'll start to see how you can accentuate your speeches with your own essence and write a presentation that is infused with YOU!

If you completed the Barrett Values Assessment and examined the PDF you were sent, you'll also see that the final page asks you which values you'd most like to demonstrate more fully in your life.

Mine were caring, risk-taking, and humour. So by adding some element of these three values into my speech preparation and delivery, I can continue to stretch myself while still satisfying my core values.

So how could I exhibit these values in my own talks?

- Caring: I could ask more questions of my audience and show the softer, more vulnerable side of my personality during anecdotes and stories.

- Humour: I love jokes, and a while back I studied stand-up comedy. I now have a better idea of how to create jokes for my talks from scratch, rather than hoping I'll randomly stumble upon some material that makes the audience laugh.

- Risk taking: I could take more risks with my content and spend less time on scripting my speeches.

In fact, early on in my speaking journey, this is exactly what I did. I was used to scripting every speech fully and had developed a painstaking process for committing the lines to memory. Later I decided to move a little closer to the edge (for a steady Virgo like me who has perfectionist tendencies, that was quite a decision—I must confess!)

I made a commitment to speak more frequently and prepare talking points. My heart beat a little faster than normal and I definitely stumbled over a few words. However, I survived the experience and learned from it. These days, I script key moments of my talks, but not every single word.

So please do go ahead and find out your core values. You might learn something surprising!

What's Your WHY?

Simon Sinek's book *Start With Why* puts forth the idea that people will identify with your *why*—your overarching mission in life—more than with your job title, goals, or any of the other detail you might share with them. Therefore, it's important to share your why—your key driver in life—preferably during the first few minutes of your talk.

The remaining detail can come later, after you've made that vital connection with the audience and created an environment of receptivity and openness. Here are some questions you can ask to help find your why:

- What is the big motivator in your life? The driver that gets you out of bed in the morning? Is it your family and children? Is it your spirituality or religious beliefs? Is it the pursuit of wealth?

- What is it that pulls you forward and gets your juices flowing, making you determined to succeed?

Once you know your why, it's important to share it when appropriate. Perhaps you mention it during your personal story, at the beginning of the talk, or during the credibility section. Or if you're giving a short piece at a networking group, briefly mention it before you describe the goods or services you offer.

By sharing your why, and the story behind it, you bond with people on an emotional level and it cuts through much of the surface detail people are picking up from you—your appearance, mannerisms—all those little things that we fickle and superficial human beings tend to dwell upon. Many of these judgements will crumble in the face of a strong and relatable why, delivered up as a personal story.

What is your key driver? How can you succinctly relate it to your audience?

One of my clients, Lesley, works as a highly paid business consultant. Financial security is very important to her. During a group session, she shared her why. She comes from a family of six children and as a youngster, there wasn't much money to go around. She now prioritises being well paid because it allows her to treat her family to luxuries that weren't accessible during her younger years.

When Lesley shared this with the other ladies in the group, they instantly warmed to her and understood exactly what motivated her to always want the best that money can buy.

Personality Profiling

Another useful test is the Myers-Briggs personality type test (www.sholakaye.com/mbf). Personality types were originally theorised by the psychologist Carl Jung and later, Isabel Briggs Myers, an American researcher, added an additional dimension. This test is used in many organisations to help better understand how employees do their best work and what motivates them.

I suggest taking the test at this site and looking at your results (www.sholakaye.com/mbt).

> **The first time I completed the Myers-Briggs test was more than two decades ago and I found it helped explain certain behaviours and preferences I had. For example, I'm a thinker. I'm also quite an introverted person. Analysing the MB results made me see that there was nothing wrong with being a naturally quiet person with a rich life going on inside my mind. It also showed me the need for activities such as meditation, which gives my brain a rest from time to time. It stops the little mouse on the wheel that represents the steady and continuous stream of thoughts running through my head.**

I love public speaking because it's a way to share ideas, to help people learn and grow. Personally, the thrill of speaking comes from the challenge of serving the audience and explaining material in new ways that they quickly and easily understand.

If you're a more extroverted type, your enjoyment of public speaking might come from making a connection through airing and sharing your views and from creating an emotional bond with the audience. Or maybe you love being the centre of attention!

Once you get your results, read the reports through thoroughly. Of particular interest is the Communication Style report.

Take a careful note of the "What Helps" and "What Hinders" sections.

After looking at my own report, my strategic, conceptual, and creative approach made sense to me. I saw that I'm better at talking about high-concepts and strategies than getting into too much detail.

You might be the total opposite. Perhaps you love contracts and granular detail.

Write down your communication 'helps and hindrances' and keep it near at hand for the next time you write a speech. It will assist you in seeing your strengths and the areas in which you might need support.

Personas – A Little Help from Your 'Friends'

I'd like to touch on the idea of using personas.

What's a persona? We are all a combination of different traits and personalities.

When I'm playing with my goddaughters, I'm fun and lively. If I'm holding a tiny baby, I'm gentle and sweet. If I'm defending someone who's been mistreated, I'm earnest and persistent. When I'm on stage singing in front of hundreds of people, I'm vocal, larger than life, and often a little bit cheeky—I love to banter with the audience.

So then the question is: Which is the 'real' Shola? The authentic me?

In reality, we are all a complex jumble of different traits. So why not call upon the traits you need at the time you need them?

During a workshop, someone once asked me, "I feel uncomfortable speaking in a loud voice when I'm on stage. Day to day, that's not how I behave. How should I deal with this?"

What I say is, have you ever needed to speak with a louder voice before? Maybe you have a hard of hearing auntie or you're on the phone and it's a poor line? So you raised your voice or projected further in order to be heard. During that moment, did you feel a fake? Probably not!

In the same way, we can assess our speaking situations and add in a sprinkle (or a dollop) of whichever trait or behaviour we need to get us the best result.

- Do you need to project your voice? Pretend you're talking to an elderly relative who is a little hard of hearing.

- You need to be fiery and energetic? Visualise cheering on your favourite team or going to a loud concert or show.

Write a list of all the different situations you regularly find yourself in, and how each one makes you behave. Then you can call on that behaviour at the appropriate point of your presentation.

For example:

> *Supporting my son when he's playing soccer:* passionate and loud
>
> *Out for a cocktail with girlfriends:* upbeat and humorous

Hopefully you'll realise that you have an array of mannerisms, voices, and demeanours at your disposal, all of which are naturally you.

It's about harnessing the energy you need. That way you can step out the self that says "I can't do it", or "It's not me", or "I'm too small for this" and be a bigger person. A person who has the energy to give to an entire group. A person who radiates what's in her heart and lets that energy touch tens, hundreds, or even thousands of people, instead of just one or two.

How do you want to be seen? What additional energy or behaviour do you want to incorporate into your speeches?

Decide when and where you might need an extra energy boost from one of your personas to help you give your best performance.

***

In this chapter, we looked at who you are, your values, and your big why. We also explored the concept of personas, helping you harness all the different facets of your personality to deliver a dynamic and exciting presentation.

DIVA CHALLENGE: What's your big WHY? Do you have a short personal story you can use in your speeches to explain its origins? If not, create one.

Now roll up your sleeves and get ready to create a wonderful talk. It's time to walk step-by-step through the speech writing process!

Part Two

Chapter 8
Writing Your Speech

How do you put together everything you've learned to create your winning speech?

Early on in my speaking days, I didn't have a routine to craft my presentations. Over time I developed a system that works for me. This is what I share with my clients to break the process down and make it straightforward.

You need to convey your message in a way that's easily understood.

Will you have handouts? If not, then it's even more important that your presentation is memorable.

I'll refer to different sections of this book where I've treated some of these points in more depth. However, this chapter gives you most of what you need to produce an effective talk that shows off you, and your material.

Some Key Questions

After you've done your audience research (see Chapter 5), it's time to sit down and ask yourself some important questions:

- What is your audience expecting to hear from you?

- What do they need to learn or find out?

- What's the main point of your talk? If you had to chunk it down into one sentence, what would that be? Is there a catchy or snappy way to summarise this? If so, create a throughline or a foundational phrase that's memorable and that you can repeat several times during the talk (for more on the **throughline**, see the Chapter 5).

- How long will you have to speak for?

- How many sub-points do you need to make?

- What are the stories you'll use to illustrate your point?

- Do you need any visual aids or diagrams?

- What's the call to action? What should the audience DO after the talk?

- What do you want the audience to FEEL after hearing your talk?

- Do you need to capture anything (business cards, email addresses, donations) from the audience as a side benefit of your appearance? How will you do this in a seamless and non-salesy way?

Get yourself a pen, a pack of sticky notes, a cup of something enjoyable, and let's go!

Using Mind Maps

Before you commit any of your content to slideware or a handout, I recommend you map out your entire presentation, first using a mind map brain dump, and later using sticky notes.

First, Create Your Mind Map:

This is a good start if you know a lot about the topic but are not sure what to include. Take a blank sheet of paper, and in the middle put the title or subject of your talk. Then, create a series of branches that extend throughout the page in all directions.

At the end of each of these branches should be one of the topics or points you might include in your talk. Write down the point and then branch off again with all the related sub-points you could include. Just write them in note form for now—no need to be too detailed. Keep writing, adding more branches as needed, until you can't think of anything more on the topic and you've expressed all your ideas. You can include hints for story titles, useful questions, statistics, anything you feel is relevant and that will help you create an effective speech.

Software programs to help with this include Coggle, Mindmeister, and SimpleMind. There are many others available, some free and some premium.

Once you've finished, take a look and decide what to include in the presentation. Circle or highlight the key points you want to keep.

The mind map should only take 5-10 minutes, provided you have a good grasp on your subject matter and know what the audience is expecting to hear. If you're struggling at this stage, then do a bit more research until you have a solid knowledge of the subject.

Now we will arrange the content and make some checks to ensure we have a DIVA presentation on our hands. Remember that we want it to be DYNAMIC, INSPIRING, VALUABLE and AUTHENTIC!

Create Your Speech

Beginning, middle, and end. Begin by first drafting the middle of your presentation and let your material suggest the best way to open and close the speech. Many people get bogged down trying to create an amazing opener and take ages to finish this section, leaving less time to get the rest of the presentation right.

Start with the meat of your talk: the middle. That way, when you come to write the opening and closing sections they will be SO much easier to construct.

Create the Middle:

- What is the content you intend to share?

- What's your throughline, when will you use it and how many times? Remember that this is the equivalent of a chorus in a song. You want the audience to hear it enough times to remember this message above all others.

- Break your content down into 3 to 5 points and assemble them in a logical order. For example, in my talk *How to be a DIVA at Public Speaking* I break my content into four parts using my DIVA framework—

Dynamic, Inspiring, Valuable, and Authentic. Another speaker on the same subject might have a talk titled *Top 5 Ways to Be A Convincing Speaker.*

- If you have a longer talk to deliver (more than 20-30 minutes), break each point into 2-5 sub-points.

- Bring the content to life by including some illustrative detail, a story or an example for each main point.

- List the questions you can ask to draw the audience in as you introduce each of these main points.

- Make a note of the information you'll display on slides, or the moments where you might write down audience responses on a flip chart.

Create the Opening:

- Select the disruptor you plan to use (to grab the audience's attention from the get-go) and craft your opening lines.

- What's your story and/or credibility statement?

- Signpost your talk. What should the audience expect to hear and how will they benefit from listening to you?

- If you want them to ask questions as you go along, make a note to tell them this near the beginning.

Create the End:

- How will you summarise your content? Make sure the ending isn't too abrupt and try to be uplifting.

- What's the moral of the story or the potential impact of taking action or following through with your suggestions?

- Will there be a Q&A? If so, remember not to put it right at the end of your talk. Take control by closing *after* the Q&A.

- Is there anyone you need to thank? Remember the A/V staff, organisers, and most importantly, the audience.

- What's the call to action and how will you convey it?

Is Your Content Inspiring?

Review Chapter 4.

- Have you peppered your talk with meaningful stories and examples that bring your content to life?

- Have you used lots of inclusive you and we language that draws people in and makes them feel you're speaking exclusively to them?

- Have you included detail about yourself that creates a bond with the audience and makes you seem like a regular person they can identify with?

- Did you make your stories accessible and interesting using the DIP or CAR frameworks, or the Hero's Journey?

Is Your Content Valuable?

Review Chapters 5 and 6. Make sure you're giving your audience the best possible experience, leaving them feeling enriched and satisfied rather than robbed of their time.

- Will your slides be clean and uncluttered?

- Are your charts or graphs simple and clear?

- Is there a flow to the information you're presenting so that each new point seems like the logical next step?

- Do you have a memorable throughline that links your material together?

- Will the audience leave with the feeling they've learned something new or had an entertaining experience?

You: Dynamic and Authentic

How do you want to come across?

- Fiery and enthusiastic?

- Calm and knowledgeable?

- Friendly and sincere?

What does it mean to you to be dynamic and authentic? If Adele walks across the stage and claps her hands, that's an energetic moment. If J-Lo were to do the same we'd know she was just getting warmed up.

Nothing is wrong with either approach. These DIVAs know their own style and stick to it.

What's Your Style?

Give yourself the opportunity to experiment a little:

- Join a speaking club and ask people what works.

- Record your talks at home or at work and explore different styles of delivery.

- Get feedback from colleagues, friends and family.

- Figure out which parts of *you* you'd like to emphasise on stage.

Tom Jackson is a live music producer (www.tomjacksonproductions.com). He's hired to plan aspects of an artist's show, including staging, lighting, movement and more. He says that audiences come to a show for 3 reasons:

1. *To be captured and engaged*

2. *To experience 'moments'*

3. *To experience a change in their lives.*

You may not want to hire Tom to stage your 20-minute talk at the local Rotary club. That doesn't stop you from doing your own mini-check on this.

Be Dynamic:

- How will you use the stage?

- What props will you use?

- What's the energy you want to convey?

- How will you communicate this with your slides, gestures, movement, and vocabulary?

- How do you want the audience to FEEL when you're done? What can you do upfront to ensure that you reach your objective?

Be Authentic:

- What's your party trick? If you have one is it appropriate to include it? It will make your talk so much more memorable.

- Which one or two of your VALUES can you convey during this talk?

- Have you included any of your own photography as background for slides? It's not difficult these days to create your own images and to upload them into your presentations. They will give the audience a better idea of who you are.

- What's your persona? Which parts of yourself will you emphasise to get the message across? Do you need to show a more caring side? Or perhaps the best approach is to project the capable expert?

- Did you include your *why* in your talk and explain your motivation? This is a sure-fire way to stamp the talk with your unique character and personality.

Using Sticky Notes

The next step is to plot your presentation using sticky notes. This essential process will save you time and focus your thinking. You can stick the notes on a whiteboard, on your wall, or even just arrange them on your desk. Make sure you have a clear, good-sized space where you can complete this.

For each slide, summarise the content on a sticky note. For section dividers or slides that will only contain an image, take a sticky note and write down what kind of image you'd like to use.

Once you've mapped out the entire presentation, move the notes around until you're happy with the order and flow of your material.

Create Your Slides or Speaking Notes

Then, go ahead and create your slides using your chosen software program. If you're not using slides, use your sticky notes to represent the sections and bullet points of your talk.

For workshops and longer presentations, I create a separate printout for myself with the presenter's notes, stories, questions, and prompts written out in bullet form. That way I know exactly what I'll say and when. I use these notes for rehearsal. At the venue I can keep the notes on a side table, just in case.

Having the notes printed out separately makes you better prepared for last minute snags. It's a step I recommend unless your speech is short or you know your material inside and out.

***

Congratulations! You should now have a working speech. Your slides (if any) should have been created, having first been mapped out for content and order using sticky notes. You should also know the main point of the speech and what action(s) you'd like the audience to take once you're done.

DIVA CHALLENGE: Think about what you want your audience to FEEL during and after your next speech. How will you accomplish this? Do you need to alter your speech delivery or change your content?

In the next chapter, we take a look at some of the places you can find speaking gigs, whether you're a beginner, a relatively experienced speaker, or a pro. We also look at some tips on how you can increase your currency on stage and be credible with your audience.

Chapter 9
Finding Speaking Gigs - A
DIVA Gets What She Needs

This short chapter covers some important areas. First, we look at the significance of building credibility with your audience and sharing your achievements.

We then explore the importance of asking your audience for what *you* need; sometimes we give a speech in the hope that the audience will buy our products or supply their contact details. However, we don't explicitly ask because we're afraid, or we think the audience would prefer us to be indirect. Why waste an opportunity by being unclear?

Finally, we take a quick look at where you can find speaking gigs. This is one of the questions I'm asked most often, so perhaps my next book will explore this in much more depth!

A DIVA Knows and Shows Her Worth – Your Story and Credentials

When I'm out gigging, the audience likes to know who I am, where I've performed, and who I've performed with. Sometimes I sing in a girl trio. The other lovely ladies have appeared in West End musicals like We Will Rock You, Chicago, and Dancing In The Streets. I find that whenever I mention my co-performers' history, there is an extra level of audience appreciation, which even translates into increased enjoyment of the show.

As speakers, too, it's important to share our credentials so the audience appreciates and respects us.

Your credentials should be stated near the beginning of the talk. You should also be seeding your talk with information that shows you in a good light. Do this using client stories, anecdotes about your accomplishments, and snippets of relevant detail. This helps build the audience's confidence in you, your content, and your credibility.

I've chosen to bring this topic up again here because, in my experience, women are often terrible at sharing their achievements with the audience.

There's absolutely nothing wrong with blowing your own trumpet a bit before launching into your talk. Before you begin, your audience will be wondering, "Who is this person? Why should I be listening to this? What's her experience in this area?" These questions will be a barrier to their ability to focus and concentrate on your talk, so it's very important to address them early on.

Sharing your credentials is doing the audience a favour. Give them a solid list of reasons why they should be listening to you, and what qualifies you to be there. Not only will it set their minds to rest, it will also make them feel honoured that they're in the presence of such an accomplished speaker, thought leader, and DIVA.

If you're feeling particularly awkward about sharing your greatness, share your big WHY or a personal story first (what motivates you, what drives you, or a tough time in your life) and then state your credentials on the back of that. People love to hear stories of triumph over adversity and will be rooting for you if you tell them what you've had to overcome.

Sometimes I share the anecdote about a former boss at a management consulting company in the USA. He told my colleagues that I was so quiet, he wondered if there was something wrong with me! I then share that I'm now an international performer. Because I reveal my vulnerability first, the audience enjoys learning about my accomplishments when I share them later on.

If you feel particularly uncomfortable sharing your credentials, write a succinct paragraph that your introducer can read out before you go on stage. For larger events, you can even create a short video to be played as an introduction. This will spare you from having to big-up yourself to the audience. They'll still learn how wonderful you are, and will know what an honour it is to hear you speak.

If you are just getting started and truly don't feel you have credentials related to your speaking topic, feel free to share any other information that will bring you closer to the audience. Perhaps you're speaking to a group of parents and you have children of your own. Share your kids' accomplishments or your pride at what they've done. If your aspirations are the same as those you're speaking to, share them. Be both humble *and* ambitious. Let them see the real you. Go back in time and share a pivotal event in your life that brought you to where you are today.

A DIVA Asks for What She Needs

You'd probably like acknowledgement for a job well done. Maybe you want to be re-booked. Perhaps you'd appreciate a standing ovation from the crowd. Great!

Going beyond that, what details do you want to capture from your audience or what actions would you like them to take as a result of your presentation?

Whatever it is you want them to DO, think this through first! A DIVA asks for what she needs. Do you want leads, referrals, email addresses, book purchases? Don't be afraid to ask for what you want. Ask with grace and poise, but ask!

It's so easy to fall into the trap of wanting to deliver a top-notch speech without planning what comes next.

If you want them to attend your next event, write your speech with that in mind. If you want them to buy your book, weave in some quotes or position the book in such a way that it's impossible for them to leave without purchasing a copy.

Of course, add value and don't make your talk a total snooze fest because it's full of plugs to buy your stuff. Seed your talk with the additional benefits you know you can provide if only they decide to take things further (see Chapters 5 and 6).

If you've done a good job with your talk, the majority of people will want to capture a piece of your action. Whether that's by signing up for your newsletter, leaving a business card so they can hear more, or buying your book, don't waste a key opportunity to take your relationship with the audience to the next level.

Where to Find Speaking Gigs – All DIVA'd Up with Nowhere to Go?

One of the questions I'm asked most often is "Where do I find speaking gigs?"

I respond with "Once upon a time, in a far-off distant land, there was a beautiful tree. With a slender trunk and abundant leaves, it was called The Speaking Gig Tree. It was fabled that people would stand beneath it, give its narrow tree trunk a shake, and all sorts of juicy, well-paid, speaking gigs would fall down around their feet. Hurrah!"

Oops . . . wake up. WAKE UP!

It's a lovely story, but I'm sorry to tell you that this tree doesn't exist. Yes, wipe the tears away and roll up your sleeves, because it takes hard work and determination to find gigs. Here are a few of the ways I've seen or used. This is by no means an exhaustive list.

- When You're Starting out

- Join Toastmasters (www.toastmasters.org) – find a club that meets frequently and doesn't have too many members. That way you'll have more opportunities to speak. There's also much to be learned from watching other speakers and listening to them being evaluated.

- Contact your local Rotary Club (www.rotary.org) or similar communities.

- Women's Institute (www.thewi.org.uk)

- Schools

- Church or other organisations you belong to

- Open mic nights

- When You Have a Bit More Experience

- Meetups (www.meetup.com) are gatherings organised all over the world and each meetup group has a particular theme. Go online and find groups in your local area that are related to your topic. *Don't just email the organiser cold.* Attend one or two of their meetings, get to know the organiser, and then ask if there are opportunities to speak.

- Create your own events and invite guest speakers. Have the speakers bring people along from their client base, get them to advertise your event to their list, or ask them to offer you a speaking slot at one of their own events.

- Multi-speaker events: you can find people with similar target markets and put on an event where all of you speak.

- Chambers of Commerce

- Networking clubs. You pay to join or to attend. They often rotate a speaking slot among the members, or you can go to different clubs within the same umbrella organisation and speak for 10 – 20 minutes. Examples are BNI (www.bni.com), Athena (www.theathenanetwork.co.uk), and many more.

- Volunteer at charities

- Run webinars

- Podcasts

- Summits

- Professional Speakers Association (www.thepsa.co.uk), National Speakers Association (www.nsaspeaker.org) and Global Speakers Federation (www.globalspeakersfederation.net). Network like crazy and make new speaker friends. Also, you might one day be invited to present at their meetings.

- Women Speakers Association (www.womenspeakersassociation.com)

- Festivals

- When You're a Pro

You might still do all of the above and also:

- Conferences

- Association events

- Corporate events

- Network with pro speakers with a similar target market. Conference organisers can't use you every year—they need to rotate their speakers—so the organisers will appreciate it if you can refer speakers of a similar calibre to yourself.

- Speaker bureaus and agencies. Don't call them; they'll call you when there's sufficient buzz about you that you can't be ignored any longer.

- Find events you like the look of, contact the organiser to ask how you can apply to speak, and see what happens.

- •! Use Google and websites like www.conferencealert.com to find events and contact the organisers.

Finding gigs can be hard work. Keep your eyes and ears open, be persistent, and keep following up. In the beginning, speak for free to get more experience. Ask the attendees to recommend other organisations and event hosts that might be able to use a speaker like you.

***

In this chapter, we looked at ways of showing your awesomeness, asking for what you need and finding a platform for your speaking.

> **DIVA CHALLENGE:** Go through the list of places to find speaking gigs and choose 3 organisations you could contact. And then, contact them within the next week!

Next, we look at how to prepare physically and mentally for your big moment on stage. Keep reading!

Chapter 10
Preparing for Showtime

So this is it! It's very nearly your time to shine. The speech is booked in and you've done your research. You've written your talk, or at the very least, have a set of well-organised bullet points to speak on. You've also thought carefully about how you'll deliver that talk and what's in it for you and the audience.

It's not about having the spotlight resting on you. A real DIVA brings the light with her.

This section looks at what should happen in the run up to your talk. It deals with everything from how to practise your talk, what to wear, what to take along with you, and even which voice exercises you can use to get your set of pipes into tip-top shape. Importantly, we also look at how to overcome nerves and fears.

Learning and Rehearsing

Most people tend to use rote learning to rehearse their speeches. I once heard a very arbitrary statement along the lines of "Remember to read your speech through at least seven times before you perform it".

That instruction seemed quite random to me. I believe we all have very different abilities when it comes to memorising or indeed, to speaking off the cuff. Both skills improve with practise. We just need to be considerate of our starting-off points.

One way to prepare for speeches is to:

- Write the whole thing out (I often prefer to script my speeches. I explore the pros and cons of this in the next section).

- Read it out loud at the pace you'd use in front of an audience.

- Remove or adjust any clunky phrases and make sure it fits to time. It's super important to never, ever go over your allotted speaking time. If you are at an event with multiple speakers, one person going overtime can derail the whole event, so be courteous and never run over unless you have permission.

- Record your speech on your phone or another device.

- Listen back when you go to bed and again first thing in the morning, and whenever you have time.

- If different phrasing and vocabulary come to you, keep making adjustments. Your speech is a living thing. Let it improve over time and don't stay fixed to your first draft.

- If there are any sections you repeatedly find difficult to remember, either alter them or practise them in isolation until you've got them down.

- Script any necessary body gestures, stage usage, facial expressions, and pauses, especially if you're telling lots of stories or jokes where the delivery is crucially important.

- Practise in front of a mirror and then in front of an audience of friends, colleagues, or peers who will give you constructive feedback. (Some speakers argue against using a mirror because it's not the same as real life. Personally I've never had a problem with it).

- Also, record on video and watch it back—you'll spot things you otherwise wouldn't have noticed.

Don't Overload Your Talk

Avoid cramming too much content into your presentation. This allows you more time for pausing, which is good for both you and the audience. Also, there will be occasions on stage where inspiration strikes and you'll want to add a few impromptu words that you hadn't prepared. Or an audience question might require that you go a little longer than you had planned to. At these times, you'll be happy you had a few unscripted moments of speaking time at your disposal.

Point-By-Point or Memorise?

A question I'm frequently asked is *should I memorise my speech word for word or use talking points?*

My answer is: It depends. Some say that you should never memorise word-for-word. In reality, many introverted speakers—some of whom get paid in the six figures to speak—have tightly rehearsed presentations that are fully scripted. On the other hand, many amazing speakers are OK with speaking off the cuff or working from a few talking points. At the beginning, you may feel more confident with a fully prepared talk. Over time you can work towards using bullets or general talking points. Do what works for you and what produces the most conversational, at-ease delivery.

Pros of Scripting the Speech:

- Your vocabulary and turn of phrase are often more interesting because you have time to select exactly the right words in advance.

- You can be confident you've included your key points (although you might still forget them on the day).

- You can rehearse the full talk and make sure it fits into the allowed time.

- This method is really good for facts, figures, and complex information that needs to be delivered in sequence. For example, jokes and quotes.

- It's good for less confident speakers who need more preparation and are afraid to 'wing it'.

Cons of Scripting the Speech:

- It takes longer to prepare.

- If you forget a sentence or two it can completely throw you off track.

- Unless you're well-rehearsed, the delivery may be less spontaneous and a bit wooden.

- You'll need enough time to memorise your words.

- It may stop you from being in the moment, especially if you haven't practised enough and are feeling shaky and uncertain.

Script Your Open and Close

Regardless of which method you choose—whether memorisation, speaking from talking points or a combination of the two—it can be useful to script and fully rehearse your opening and also your close. These are the sections people remember best so you need to make an impact here and not leave anything to chance.

You can also use visual techniques like **the memory palace** to help you remember your points. There are lots of videos on YouTube that go into this in more depth (www.sholakaye.com/palace). Just search for 'memory palace' and you'll find them!

A DIVA is well-prepared

I'd been asked to sing at a rather nice wedding up at one of the top hotels in Glasgow, and the bride had suggested I wear an outfit she'd seen in one of my videos. It was a red silk dress that I'd had made to order.

On the day I was due to fly to Scotland, I took out my dress (that I'd not worn in a few months) and realised it had a small stain on it. Right on the front and in the middle. Ouch.

It definitely wasn't in a wearable state. I ended up performing in a dress that was a similar colour, but not the one the bride had requested. She was kind enough to say nothing on the day, but I saw her look at me a couple of times and I'm sure she noticed it wasn't her choice.

I felt guilty and awkward that I'd not provided what I'd been asked for, especially for such an important occasion in the bride and groom's life.

So, lesson learned. Be prepared!

If you're travelling far from home then bring an alternative outfit, just in case, or change when you arrive.

There are other items we need to prepare. This section deals with those, so read on.

Breathing

If you're a speaker, singer, or actor, you'll have encountered a huge amount of advice related to breathing techniques. Before I started performing seriously, I used to wonder what all the fuss was.

The reason it's so important is because we can use our breath to control our performance.

Have you ever had a scare and experienced your fight, flight or freeze response? If so, your sympathetic nervous system has kicked in. This is the part of our nervous system that causes our heart to beat faster and our digestion to slow down. Extra blood is pumped to the muscles, giving us the energy to run or fight.

A colleague recently had a brush with a motorbike while she was crossing the road. A gutsy, confident woman with tons of energy, she was shocked to find herself in freeze mode as the bike ran into her in the middle of the street. Luckily, she escaped with cuts and bruises. Later, she explained how disappointed she was that her instinct had been to freeze, rather than to flee.

That's the problem. We aren't in control of how we respond.

The same applies to public speaking. If we fail to take precautions to guard against nerves, they can crop up in a variety of ways: sweaty palms and face, shaking hands, the mind going blank. It's no wonder people are afraid of public speaking if they've no idea what kind of uncontrollable reaction they have in front of a group of strangers.

On the other hand, when we are relaxing and enjoying a quiet moment—maybe lying on the sofa at home, or in the park in the sun—our parasympathetic nervous system (which is responsible for our rest and digest responses) kicks in instead. The parasympathetic nervous system (PSNS) works to save us energy. Blood pressure decreases and our pulse rate slows down.

The PSNS is stimulated by relaxed breathing. Steady, natural breathing increases the supply of oxygen to our brain and promotes calmness. It will also reduce anxiety and stress. The PSNS and the sympathetic nervous system can't be activated at the same time—it's one or the other.

So this is why it's so important to breathe naturally, even when you're feeling anxious and scared.

The process of natural breathing leads to relaxation.

If you are particularly fearful of speaking then you might even want to start a meditation practice, focused on the breath. There are many good apps for this, examples include www.headspace.com, www.calm.com, and www.buddhify.com. After a short while, you'll be able to breathe naturally on demand and perhaps even find that your public speaking anxiety disappears.

Try this: stand up straight with your arms by your sides, relax, and breathe naturally. No need to take a huge deep breath—don't try to cram yourself with air! Just breathe gently and naturally.

After a few cycles of inhalations and exhalations, place one hand on your waist and another on your upper chest. As you breathe in you should feel your waistline expand while your upper chest only moves very slightly, if at all. The breath should be nice and low.

Now put one hand on your rib cage and another on your back. Keep breathing naturally. You should feel both your ribcage and back expand as you breathe gently and calmly.

You'll find more on breathing in the book's online resources (www.sholakaye.com/divabookcourse).

Power Posing

Amy Cuddy, the Harvard psychologist, has done some research which shows that if you allow your body to take on certain stances or **power poses**, the body releases testosterone—the hormone that creates feelings of confidence—and reduces the stress hormone, cortisol. So if you put your hands on your hips with your legs planted firmly, shoulder-width apart—like Wonder Woman—and hold the pose for two minutes, you'll likely feel more self-assured and powerful.

Try this exercise immediately before you rehearse or speak and see if it works for you. If it does, incorporate it into your daily morning routine or pop into the loo before you speak and take two minutes to stoke up your presentation superpowers.

Dealing with Nerves

Many people have issues with the fear of public speaking or *glossophobia*.

So far I've tried not to mention that certain polls in the USA report that people fear public speaking ahead of fears of death and of spiders (www.sholakaye.com/poll). But aah, I couldn't resist it! In addition, some 74% of people suffer from some sort of speech anxiety (www.sholakaye.com/74).

So here are a few ways to deal with nerves. Every person is different, so choose what works for you.

Reframe It

Don't say you're suffering from fear and nerves. Instead, refer to it as excitement!

The energy you experience as a presenter is very similar to the sensations sports competitors feel before they go out to run their big race. Your body is getting ready to access the energy it needs to get through your performance. You may experience that as a faster heartbeat, shaky hands, sweaty palms, or butterflies in the stomach.

The key is your interpretation of these feelings. Choose to label them as something positive, and you'll look forward to speaking. Label them as negative, and you'll be like the character in the Seinfeld sketch that would rather have been in the hearse than delivering the eulogy.

Tell yourself "Wow, I'm so excited about this amazing opportunity to share my words with these people. I can't wait to connect with them and hopefully change their lives. I'm relaxed and happy, and all I want is for it to go well and for the audience to be blown away by the experience."

Think Positive and Ask Empowering Questions

If I tell you to think of an orange cow, most likely, that's what will pop into your head. In the same way, if you run a script through your mind of everything that could potentially go wrong, it will fill your head and there'll be no space left for positivity and thoughts of success.

That's why it's really important to crowd out the negativity with thoughts of doing well and having a great result.

It's easier said than done because our human minds are pre-wired to focus more on the negative than the positive. This harkens back to our caveman ancestors who could potentially have died if they didn't take care of the details.

- Do they have food? (No Tesco Metro nearby for them if they don't manage to chase down some unfortunate beast for that day's dinner).

- Do they have shelter? (Maybe they're on the way to the next camp and can't risk nightfall in the open).

- Do they have protection? (If they get separated from the group or ostracised, then most likely game's up because they won't survive alone).

Flash forward thousands of years to the moments before a speech, and we're thinking: "What if the audience doesn't like me?" And our prehistoric lizard brain interprets the outcome as *maybe I'll be ostracised and left alone to die.*

Extreme reaction, yes!

"What if I screw up?" Lizard brain thinks *maybe I'll be rejected by everyone and left alone to die.*

"What if my slide-show doesn't display correctly?" Lizard brain thinks *maybe I'll be cast out of the community and left alone to die.*

You get the idea!

So the key is to replace these niggly, needly, negative fears with positive statements and empowering questions.

Use **questions** like:

- What if it goes really, really well?

- What can I do to make this talk even better?

- How can I connect with the audience?

Think **statements** such as:

- I love to speak, what a great opportunity this is!

- I've done all the preparation I can on this speech and I'm ready!

- I can't wait to serve my audience and help them by giving them this useful information.

If you're a worrier (like me), you can write these positive statements down and read them whenever you have a spare moment. You can also create a positive recording on your phone and play it before you go to bed.

Write down at least fifteen positive questions full of possibility, such as:

- How will I feel after this goes really well?

- How can I do an amazing job?

- What are my main strengths when it comes to speaking?

And include positive statements too:

- My audience will adore this talk.

- I've put all my creativity and energy into this and it'll be amazing.

- I'm going to enjoy giving this speech. It's on my favourite subject!

Record them onto your phone. If you have software like Audacity or Garageband you can record the statements on your computer and repeat them so you have a loop of an hour or so of positive messages to lull you off to sleep. Even while you're snoozing, your brain will continue to absorb this empowering content. It's a very effective way of boosting your confidence and enthusiasm.

Visualise Success

Shakti Gawain's book, *Creative Visualisation*, was originally published in 1978. Since then the process of visualisation has become a worldwide movement, adopted by sports psychologists, performers and business people alike.

Olympians such as Jessica Ennis, winner of the heptathlon during the UK's recent Summer Olympic Games and Michael Phelps, the most decorated Olympian swimmer of all time, swear by the practise.

The brain can't tell the difference between the experience itself, and a richly textured, highly detailed visualisation. So by running the perfect picture through our minds before the big day, we're helping to create the conditions for success.

The key is to imagine your speaking gig in great detail, seeing the entire event running perfectly from start to finish. In the online course that accompanies this book, there is an audio version of a visualisation that I created for your use. Play it back regularly ahead of your talk.

If you can't visit the venue of your talk before the day, ask the organiser to send you a photo of the speaking area and the room so you can include an accurate picture in your visualisation process.

Guided Visualisation for Public Speaking

(Found at www.sholakaye.com/divabookcourse)

Sit quietly with your back supported. Allow yourself to relax and feel gravity acting on your body. Breathe naturally and slowly for a few moments.

Inhale through your nose, allowing your lungs to gently fill with air, and then slowly exhale through your mouth. Repeat at the same relaxed pace.

Inhale. Exhale. Inhale. Exhale.

While you continue to breathe calmly and naturally, imagine yourself on stage at the speaking venue.

As you stand in front of the audience, imagine the scene becoming brighter and the colours growing more vivid. Your body is relaxed and attentive, and you're feeling more and more confident, full of power and determination. Think to yourself, *"I can do this! I'm here to serve my audience and I'm fully prepared."*

Now picture the audience sitting in front of you. They're all eager to hear you speak, they want you to be a huge success. You know you can satisfy them with your inspiring stories, useful information, and dynamic, authentic presence.

Now, hear yourself speak. The sound of your voice is rich and resonant. You take your time, go at your own pace, and enjoy every moment. Your body language is genuine and expressive. As you make eye contact with the audience, they listen attentively. When you ask questions, their hands go up in eager response. It feels wonderful, and you have everyone in the palm of your hand. Finally, as you come to a close, the audience jump to their feet and give you a standing ovation. What a success! You smile and absorb the applause and the positive energy. You were great!!!

Create an Anchor for Your Success

This exercise will allow you to draw on past positive experiences to help you create a powerful mental, physical, and emotional state when you give your speech.

1. Recall a time when you were feeling confident and successful. Make the memory clear and vivid. How did you feel? What did you see? What did you hear? What did you smell?

2. When the memory is very clear in your mind and you feel as if you were there in the moment, activate a physical trigger. This trigger should be something that

no one else notices, such as touching a thumb and forefinger together or making a fist.

3. Repeat steps one and two, using the same memory, or use a combination of different positive memories to reinforce the anchor.

4. Test the anchor by using the trigger you chose, for example, by clenching your fist. You should find that your state of mind changes and the feelings of confidence and success come surging back.

5. Repeat your anchor daily, because it will become stronger with consistent use. Try to start this practice at least a week or two before your presentation. Continue to strengthen your anchor by repeating steps one and two.

6. When you come to deliver your speech, make that same anchor gesture just before you go on stage. Allow the confident feelings to come flooding back. Complete your talk in a powerful mental, physical, and emotional state.

Vocal Warm Ups and Tongue Twisters

Speaking is a physical activity. Just as an athlete trains and warms up before the big race, it's important to do the same before your big presentation.

Vocal warm ups. I already mentioned the *mmm* sound back in Chapter 3 on being a DYNAMIC speaker. This is one of my favourite vocal warm-ups.

Try making the *mmm* sound for a minute, with breaths in between, of course. We don't want you fainting before you even get on stage for the talk.

Here are some other things to try:

- Place your hand on your rib cage and breathe naturally. Your rib cage should expand when you inhale and contract when you exhale. Try this for a minute or two. Inhale to the count of four. Then hold for two. Exhale to the count of four. Hold for two. Repeat.

- Drink water in the hours leading up to your talk. It's not good enough to take a sip or two while waiting to speak. Make sure your vocal cords are properly hydrated.

- Exercise your tongue:

  o Extend it out of your mouth as far as possible straight ahead.

  o Lower it to touch your bottom lip.

  o Stretch it up to touch your top lip.

  o Stretch it to the left of your mouth to touch the skin on your face just beyond the edge of your mouth.

  o Repeat the above on the right side.

Tongue twisters. These are also very useful. If there are particular letters of the alphabet or sounds you struggle with you can use Dr. Google to find appropriate exercises. Don't feel you need to rush through them. Sound them out slowly, with care and resonance. Use the vowel sounds to warm up the voice and the consonants to sharpen your articulation.

I have included several videos for warming up the voice in the online course. Run through them daily to get your voice in peak condition for speaking.

Your Clothes

I'd rocked up to perform at a little venue in Portsmouth, on the south coast of the UK. It was two hours before the show and I was dressed casually in blue jeans and a stripy T-shirt. People were already at the venue, drinking at the bar, and I felt a few eyes upon me as I set up my gear, but thought nothing of it.

A couple of hours later, it was showtime. I ran out on stage wearing my Diana Ross wig and a red, sequined, off-the-shoulder dress and heard someone in the front row say, in a very loud voice, "Oh, she scrubs up well!"

Was that a compliment or an insult? Were my jeans and T-shirt really so bad that they created a low expectation of my stage clothing? I didn't let it bother me. However, the experience shows that people are judging you by your appearance from the minute you arrive at a venue.

Nowhere does that happen more than when you are giving a speech. You are the star attraction. People don't have anywhere else to look. For sure, all eyes will be upon you so dress appropriately and have no regrets.

For example, health blogger Kris Carr says that when she's public speaking "This is the one time I make an effort to gussie up like a classy pro".

As a DIVA, I trust you to make your own judgement on what to wear. One rule of thumb is to dress the same as, or a bit smarter than the audience. So that's another question for your audience research.

Will it be a black-tie affair or is it more casual? Whatever the answer, give yourself enough time to prepare. Check your outfit a few days before in case it needs a spell at the dry cleaner or there's a thread that needs to be cut off or sewn in.

If it's a business presentation, consider your brand colour. The Speak up like a DIVA brand is orange, and there is also some pink and maroon in the logo. I try to wear one of these colours, or second best, some red, when I speak. It gives the audience something bright to look at and also increases brand awareness, even if this happens on a more subconscious basis.

Some speakers have a signature outfit they wear every time, regardless of the audience. There are speakers who always wear jeans, others who always wear trainers. Some only wear trouser suits and others always wear a dress. Once you've developed your own style and it's successful, don't be afraid to let that become part of your regular appeal.

The most important thing is to be comfortable so you can give your best performance and not be worried by sweat patches, wrinkly clothing, too-high heels, or whatever it may be. Know yourself and decide accordingly.

***

So the moment is nearly here. In this chapter, you explored key ways to prepare for your talk, both mentally and physically.

DIVA CHALLENGE: Make a list of 10 empowering questions and statements. Record them on your phone or other device and listen to them at least once a day for the next week.

In the next chapter, we look at your live performance. We discuss how to approach the stage, what to do if you suffer from an attack of nerves, and what to analyse once your talk is done. You've come this far so don't stop now.

Because it's **showtime!**

Chapter 11
Showtime and Beyond

You've made it this far and now it's time to be seen, heard and fabulous! In this chapter, we take you to the stage to deliver your talk. We discuss what happens immediately after the talk, and how you can analyse your presentations so you are continually growing and learning from your speaking experiences.

Before the Show

Remember that a DIVA is always prepared. That's why, before the show, you should have a checklist of what to get done, what to take with you, and what to look out for.

Here are some of the items I check on for before I speak. Downloadable checklists are available online. (www.sholakaye.com/divabookcourse)

- Take my own USB remote slide advancer.

- Check if I'll be advancing the slides myself or will I get audio-visual support.

- Put the slides on a separate USB drive, email slides to the organiser (if appropriate) and have a backup copy on the cloud just in case. You may prefer not to share the slides with the organisation, so this is something to discuss with them early on and may even be a contractual issue.

- If you've used any fancy fonts in your presentation and it's playing on **their** computer, be careful as the fonts may not be installed and you might well lose your formatting.

- Check whether there's a lectern and whether I'll be required to use it.

- Check if I have to take my own laptop or if there'll be one there.

- If I do, I usually bring along my own HDMI and/or VGA cable just in case (yes, I'm paranoid!).

- If there's a mic, check what kind it is: lapel, handheld?

- Is there some way I can video the performance? Maybe take my own camera and lapel mic, or get a friend in the audience to record it for me. If it's just for your own analysis there's no need for anything fancy. A phone recording will do.

At the Venue

- Get there early. If possible, go to the stage area and look at the rows of seating from the vantage point of the speaker. If it's possible, ask the organiser to send you a photo of the stage area long before your show, so there are no surprises.

- Walk around and get a feel for how much space you have.

- If you're using slides, figure out where to stand so you don't get in the way of the visuals.

- Hook up your laptop and USB advancer (if taken) and make sure everything works.

- If there's a mic, make sure it works.

- If there's no mic, try to determine how much you'll need to project your voice to be heard at the back.

Walk among the Audience and Shake a Few Hands

If it's at all possible, mix and mingle with the audience before your talk. Shake hands with people and introduce yourself. Create a bond with the audience even before you go on stage. It can make you feel more comfortable and will help you see the audience members as friendly individuals rather than a hostile pack. The audience will often warm to you and be more receptive of your speech if you greet them first. Meeting organisers appreciate it too!

During the Show

Remember again that your audience wants you to do well. There's no more time to research, rehearse, or memorise any points.

What will be will be.

Now it's time to put yourself in a confident state so you can enjoy your presentation, serve your audience, and achieve your goals, whether it's to sell, to educate, to entertain or more.

You'll have decided how you want your audience to feel so the time is here to make sure you're feeling invigorated and ready, summoning the energy and charisma you need to work your magic on stage.

Stepping Up and Stepping Out

I always encourage my clients to create a little ritual for the moment before they present.

If you're feeling nervous and are seated in the audience directly before speaking, opportunities for last minute warm ups are limited, so the main thing I encourage you to do is the "shake it off" exercise.

Shake It off

I'm a relatively calm person and every time I'm around someone who has a nervous tic, like jiggling their leg or tapping their finger on the table, it makes me feel uneasy. However, doing the **shake it off** exercise is one time that I try to mimic that behaviour!

In your seat, as you feel the wave of nerves surge through your body, get rid of it in the following way:

Lift your heel off the ground and shake your leg as though you're trying to keep warm on a freezing cold day. Keep going with this until your nerves start to subside.

Or, under the table or in your seat, with the balls of your feet on the floor and your heels lifted slightly off the ground, you can shake your knees towards and away from each other really fast.

Approaching the Stage

When your name is called to come up and speak, don't rush to the stage in a crazy panic. It shows the audience that you're either very nervous or too keen. Slow down! Keep cool, calm, and collected.

An exercise I like comes from Caroline Goyder's book, *Gravitas*.

Imagine you're a huge dragon with an enormously long, and extremely heavy tail. There's no way you can walk fast . . . the tail slows you down and you're constantly aware of it whenever you move. It stabilises you, grounds you, and steadies you.

As you stand up to approach the stage, visualise this tail, and send thoughts of appreciation towards it. Walk slowly and steadily to the stage. There's no hurry. And you can't rush . . . your tail is taking care of that.

Eye Contact and Looking For Supporters

Once you're on stage, I encourage you to take a moment to look at the audience. You really don't have to start speaking the second you get there, and even worse is starting to talk as you're walking on unless that's your intention and it's all planned. Some presenters take 3 to 5 seconds to peruse the audience before they begin speaking. To my mind, when I see someone doing that, it's like having a big sign above their head saying 'rookie speaker'. So take your time, but don't take too long!

During these first few moments, take a deep and slow breath. It's impossible to be nervous while you're breathing slowly. While you're doing this, look at the audience and make eye contact. Where are your colleagues and supporters? Where are the friendly faces of strangers who are smiling at you and wanting you to succeed? Where are the people you chatted to or made contact with prior to the talk? Instead of seeing the audience as a sea of faces, recognise that it's a collection of individuals, each with their own opinions, thoughts, hopes, and dreams. They're not out to get you. They're giving you the precious gift of their time and attention, and your job is to serve them.

You can even imagine that your dearest friends and family are there. Visualise them sitting proudly with smiles on their faces, waiting for you to speak. Smile back at them warmly.

And begin.

If You Need to Use Notes

Have you ever seen a singer reading from a lyric sheet on stage? I try to avoid that where possible. Having to break off eye contact with the audience to look at what to sing next is a downer for me. I prefer to be connected to the viewers at all times, smiling, gesturing, and communicating. If I have to look down at lyrics, it breaks to flow.

As a speaker it's still preferable to speak without notes. However, it's also perfectly acceptable to use them. If you're at a lectern, you can even use a full transcript, especially for a long speech.

If you do need to use brief notes and won't be at a lectern, write a few bullet points on several small 3x5 inch cards. Keep these in your hand. If there's a lectern you can rest them on, you can always pop back from time to time to remind yourself of what's next. Have several cards with large handwriting you can easily read.

Don't ever take sheets of paper on stage unless you're at a lectern. It looks horribly unprofessional and it's difficult to find your place again once you glance away from your notes.

If you're speaking at a lectern, you can also put your notes on a tablet device. Remember to turn off notifications! Look up frequently to make eye contact with your audience. Make sure you can leaf through any sheets of paper silently and unobtrusively. Exercise books are a no-no because it's difficult to turn the pages without making any noise.

If You Get a Bout of Nerves

A couple of years ago, I was booked to do a show at an 800-seater theatre in Southern Europe. I knew there would be different nationalities present—very few native Brits or English speakers, and mainly Germans, Italians, Spanish, and a few Argentines. I was worried about how I'd be received by such a mixed audience. As the red velvet curtains parted and I stepped out into the spotlight in front of the packed auditorium, I had a bout of nerves. My head was ringing with all sorts of panicky questions:

- Can I handle this?

- What if I bomb?

- What if they hate it and start walking out?

- Should I be worried about this?

At that moment, I did a quick visualisation that helped me move out of my head and fully into my performance.

Thankfully, at the end of the show, there were cheers and even a few people on their feet clapping. I attribute getting through that performance to the **Hara Point** exercise that follows. You can use it at short notice and it will almost literally give you some fire in your belly to complete your presentation.

The Hara Point Visualisation

There is a point in the belly region, about an inch below your navel and an inch or two in the direction of your spine towards your back. The Japanese call it the **Hara** and they suggest that this area is the seat of your power and strength.

In actual fact, the gut is sometimes known as the second brain. It has a huge number of neurons and nerve endings running into it. That's why there are so many expressions like 'trust your gut', 'gut reaction' and why we sometimes feel butterflies in that part of the body.

When you feel nervous, think of a tiny pilot light burning at your Hara point. Whenever you need to, you can increase the energy here by visualising the little pilot light becoming a swirling ball of fire in your gut, giving you power and confidence and sending energy and light radiating throughout your entire body.

YOU are on fire!

Nobody can stop you. You have everything you need within you to do a fantastic job and to appear strong, confident, and dynamic. Feel the heat coursing through your body, providing you with the energy to give an amazing performance. Your eyes are bright with anticipation and the audience is in for a treat!

Enjoy It!

Years ago, before my first ever gig, I was extremely nervous. I'd never performed on stage before, or at least, not since I was six and attended the local dance school. This was completely different. I was fronting a band for the very first time, many of my friends would be in the audience and I *so* wanted to do well.

An old friend, Paul, gave me the best advice I'd ever heard: "Enjoy it! Forget everything else and have a good time!"

And I say that to you now.

Try your best to enjoy your time on stage. Be in the present moment. Step outside of your head and serve the audience.

Be so unconcerned about your performance that you live in the radiant now and allow a stream of the divine DIVA energy to move through you and to provide the audience with exactly what *they* need.

It's a balancing act, I know. To remember what you want to say. To move dynamically about the stage without stiffening like a robot or slouching like a reluctant teenager. To make lingering eye contact and not be thrown off track by a penetrating glance or a frown from an audience member. To know your visuals off by heart so you don't need to read the slides. To be your authentic self while you anxiously want to do a great job. To try to sell a product, service, or idea that's vital to your career and business, all the while being friendly and relaxed.

Yes, it's not easy. But remember that you're there to serve— the audience, yourself and your business if you have one. Be confident that you'll do the best you can. Put a smile on your face and get on with it. An audience can be very forgiving and you're more likeable if you come across relaxed and real. That means not trying too hard. That means putting the work in *before* the presentation day so you can enjoy the presentation itself.

No Apologies and No Excuses

A few months ago, I was in the audience at a large jazz venue in London, waiting to see a popular singer. The room was packed with diners at the supper club-style location, and many were paying top dollar to be there. The singer was running very late, and eventually, there was an announcement that she'd been held up in traffic.

After more than an hour of delay, she appeared on stage in a flustered state and proceeded to apologise profusely for what seemed like 3 or 4 minutes. Of course, it was courteous of her to apologise. But what would have gone down better would have been to launch straight into an amazing performance.

Then, later in the show, she could have taken a minute or two to share, conversationally, what had happened and how regretful she was.

Seek to establish rapport first and to give the audience what they're waiting for. Once the crowd is eating out of your hand, backtrack and make a brief apology or statement about what has gone on.

Don't give excuses—be brilliant instead.

Dealing with Difficult Subject Matter

If you're sharing a traumatic event or a serious loss, it can be difficult to complete the presentation without becoming emotional. It's OK to be moved during your talk. If the content is so raw that you genuinely don't know if you can finish without breaking down and being unable to continue, then rewrite or remove the difficult parts so you're not so easily triggered. The audience will still see that you're deeply affected. However, to break down weeping during a talk is not appropriate. Remember you're there to be of service and that means being able to complete your speech from start to finish.

Be Ready for Anything

Be prepared for audio-visual problems. Maybe your slides are not compatible with the venue's hardware or software, or maybe the projector stops working and now the slides you took ages to prepare are useless.

Make sure you're ready for any eventuality.

What would you do if your slide show didn't work? Apologise profusely and tell the audience you couldn't continue?

This is a cop-out. You have to know your content well enough that if the laptop with your slides blew up mid-speech, you could carry on without missing a beat, and make a little joke about it too!

- •! Do you know your presentation well enough that you could bring it to life without the visuals?

- •! Are there some insightful questions you can ask that will keep the audience engaged without pictures and text?

- •! Do you have some vivid stories that will take the audience on a journey?

Remember that most people are visual, so if for some reason you can't access your audio-visual material, you may need to ramp up your stage movement, descriptive storytelling and vocal variety (for the auditory individuals in the audience) to fill the gap. Go to Chapters 3, 4 and 5 for more on this.

I'd been hired to perform at the Christmas party of an international computer peripherals company and I was on stage in front of a couple of hundred people. The drinks had been flowing and many in the audience were in the party mood. I called up four audience members to join me on stage for an audience participation exercise. Unfortunately, one of them—a young guy in his early twenties—got a little too friendly on stage and in his drunken state, started groping my derriere.

Of course, it wasn't what I'd expected, nor was it what I'd been paid for! Rather than make a scene and scream like an outraged Victorian schoolmistress, I made a joke of it and kept the audience smiling until the security came and took the intoxicated offender to a quiet place where he could dry out.

Be ready for anything to happen. It probably won't, but it may do. In the run-up to a presentation, I tell people to *visualise the best and prepare for the worst*.

What's the Best Way to Be Ready for the Unexpected?

The best way to prepare for the unexpected is to stay in the present moment. Make sure you know your topic well enough that you can give your talk and be fully aware of your audience at the same time. Any speaker hired to do a TED talk (not TEDx) is required to learn their speech by heart and is even assigned a project manager to help ensure this takes place. The TED organisers want their speakers to be fully present during the talk, not in their heads trying to remember what comes next.

It's fine to speak point by point if you don't need to memorise your presentation. Just make sure you're in the moment so you can acknowledge anything that happens in the room.

If a digger starts up outside, say "And the construction workers outside agree with everything I'm saying!"

If the lights flicker on and off during a key moment, say "Aha! The powers above want me to emphasise the next point."

Create a special experience with your audience. Be spontaneous, creative, and acknowledge what goes on rather than ignoring it. It's a key moment to make a connection and they'll admire your ability to think on your feet.

Lap Up the Applause

Once your presentation is done, don't spoil it for you and for everyone else by running back to your seat like a frightened mouse.

Stand and enjoy the acknowledgement from the audience. It's really important to let them honour you fully before you leave the stage. Remember that a speech is a two-way thing. It's a conversation. You speak and the audience listens. They are, however, participating with hands up, nods and of course with their interest, as you progress through your presentation.

The applause is the audience's chance to thank you. They get the last word in your conversation. It would be rude to cut someone off if they're speaking to you. In the same way, it's impolite to rush off the stage before the bulk of the applause is over.

Plant your feet firmly on the ground at shoulder width, so you are stable and secure. Smile warmly (not triumphantly nor apologetically) and take what's yours. Make strong eye contact so the audience can see you really do appreciate their acknowledgement. You should go to your seat only when you feel the energy of the applause start to diminish and the volume dies down.

Remember your dragon tail at this point, slowing you down and grounding you as you move purposefully without rushing, and leave the stage.

Your work is done.

YES!!!! Savour the feeling. There's nothing like the overwhelming sensations of relaxation and relief that you experience immediately after giving a speech.

After the Show

Once your talk is done, it's always a good idea to mingle with the audience. This is a key time to receive feedback on your talk, listen to any questions that you weren't able to entertain from the stage and to make some great new contacts. It's also a good time to lap up praise from people who enjoyed what you had to say.

You might feel a strong urge to leave, particularly if the talk didn't go as well as you had hoped. Try to stay if you can, especially if you don't have team members present helping you collect leads and follow-ups. Override your instincts and mingle for a while.

Years ago, I was booked to sing on a cruise to Cape Town. It was for a cruise company that caters to the over 50s. This age group is notorious for being picky about what they listen to and although the cruise company tried hard to feed them new acts, their passengers were often dissatisfied and weren't afraid to show it. I performed on two separate occasions, and I remember that after the first, I headed down for breakfast the next morning. Walking among the tables of people who'd heard me sing the night before was like running the gauntlet. If they'd enjoyed the show, they would smile warmly and say hello. If they hadn't liked my set they would give me dirty looks or turn their backs to me. So if you think it's bad news to have to mingle with the audience for a half hour, try having to live with them on a cruise ship for 10 days!

On the positive side, many times you'll realise the audience enjoyed your talk more than they showed. Other times, someone will offer a great suggestion on how to make improvements. Listen to as much as you have time for and interact fully.

From time to time, people will give you advice you don't want to use. Maybe they have an axe to grind or their own agenda. Just smile, nod, receive it all gracefully, and choose to ignore it or make a mental note of what's been said and come back to it later.

This is also a great time for people to talk to you about potential new business, to get to know you a little better or to share that they'd like to chat to you further. Stay open, smiling and receptive, and keep a stash of business cards in your hand, especially if the purpose of your talk was to generate more opportunities. Also, if you have a sign-up sheet or have asked for their business cards, it's time to collect them now.

Post-Gig Analysis

After every speaking gig, it's a good idea to take a few moments to reflect on what went well and what could go better next time.

- What were the numbers like?

- Could you change your speech title to attract a bigger audience, or have a core promise attached to your talk?

- Could you advertise any bonuses or freebies to entice more people to come along?

- Where did you excel?

- How was your delivery?

- Did you make a strong connection with the audience?

- How many people wanted to speak to you after your talk?

- Were they smiling and complimenting you or did they ask questions like "Did you enjoy it?" That particular question is often a cover when the person doesn't have any glowing praise and so tries to deflect the attention back to you.

- Did you get the leads, sign-ups, sales you wanted?

- If not, was your call to action strong enough?

- Did you seed enough during the talk? Did you include enough client stories?

- Were your own stories inspiring?

- Did you honestly provide enough value?

- Do you need to update your content or make it more relevant?

When people approach and start telling you their own stories, it's usually a very good sign. It means that you touched and inspired them and that they saw themselves in you, or maybe they think you have the solution to their problem.

Watch the Video of Your Talk and Ask Yourself:

- How were your posture, stage movement, and delivery?

- Was there sufficient vocal variety?

- How was your eye contact?

- Was the pace comfortable or did you go too fast or slow?

- Did the presentation seem to flow or were there any clunky sections that felt uncomfortable?

- Did people seem engaged? Did they raise their hands in response to your questions, laugh at your jokes, and participate in the Q&A? If not, why not?

- How much did you forget? Even the most seasoned speakers forget a few words here and there so don't be hard on yourself if you did the same. Make a note for next time.

- Were there other areas you were particularly happy with?

- What do you need to work on for the next presentation?

Rate yourself out of 10, or use poor, fair, good.

Give yourself a pat on the back for your hard work, and list all the commendable points about your performance. Write down a few key areas for improvement.

If you have the stomach for it, ask colleagues, friends, family, and people in your target market to watch the video too. Listen to their responses without being defensive. There may be something vital you missed that next time could be the key to a standing ovation or a business-winning presentation. Soak up any praise and commendations people give you. Write these positive points down and read them through several times before the next presentation. This will help build up your confidence.

DIVA CHALLENGE: Next time you make a speech, record it on video (if necessary, ask an audience member to help) and then go through the checklist above to assess your performance.

***

Wow! Hopefully, by now you've created your talk, delivered it, and analysed the show. It's time to enjoy a relaxing moment with your feet up!

You've made it, DIVA!

And the more you speak, the better you'll get—so this is just the beginning.

Whatever the outcome of your talks, keep improving, keep working at it, keep applying these techniques, and there'll be no stopping you!

I'm SO glad you made it this far.

Remember, there are online resources to help you grow and improve on your speaking journey. Watch the videos for a quick reminder of the system, download the workbook and listen to the audio content.

Thanks for coming on this journey with me.

You are a star!

Conclusion – Being A DIVA

What's next?

Well, my lovely DIVA, I hope you found this book useful. If you're just starting out, you may not be able to incorporate all of the advice in this book immediately. As you gain experience in one area, select others to work on. Your speaking will grow stronger and stronger and you'll become much more confident.

I want you to be a hit at public speaking. I want you to be the speaking goddess that you were born to be. Remember that some of the best speakers were not born with the gift of the gab. They had to work at it and study their craft. It's OK to be a quiet person and speak, just as it's OK to be a naturally chatty speaker.

In this book, you discovered how to be a well-rounded presenter using the DIVA Speaking System™. Now you know how to be **DYNAMIC, INSPIRING, VALUABLE** and **AUTHENTIC** during your presentations.

You also learned how to **create your speech**, what to **prepare for a hit performance** and how to rock the stage at **show time**. It's important to keep growing on your speaking journey and you can do this by **analysing your performances**, so don't forget this step.

You also have access to written, video and audio resources to help you on your way. If you haven't done so yet, remember to go to the online course.

The key is to keep working on what you have, to keep improving, and to stay humble. It's an honour for an audience to give you their time and attention. These are precious minutes or even hours that they'll never get back. Respect that fact by preparing fully using the DIVA Speaking System™ and the information in Part Two of this book.

If you enjoyed it and would like to find out more, please do check out www.sholakaye.com for live events, online courses and the chance to work with me 1-2-1 on Skype or in person.

Remember that you have what it takes, and you have *every* right to be on stage.

If, like me, you were waiting for years for someone to tell you how wonderful you could be and to give you permission to shine, then the moment is here.

I give you permission to shine your light, speak your truth and be a DIVA at public speaking!

Warm wishes,

Shola

Thank You

Thanks so much for coming along on the DIVA journey. I sincerely hope you found it useful!

If you enjoyed the book I'd love it if you would provide me with a short review on Amazon. It will be helpful to other readers to explain what was useful to you or what you learned.

I'm passionate about women having the tools and the confidence to speak up and I would be so grateful for your help in getting the word out there to others.

If you have any feedback or questions about the book, I'd love to hear from you. Please use the contact form on my website. **(www.sholakaye.com/contact)**

If you have questions about the free online resources you're very welcome to interact with me via the course contact page. **(www.sholakaye.com/divabookcourse)**

About the Author

Shola Kaye is an award-winning public speaker, an international singer, and founder of the training company Speak Up Like A DIVA.

She was born in London and from a young age wanted to be a performer, but instead studied Natural Sciences at Cambridge University and then trained to be a teacher at Merton College, Oxford.

While Shola was working at a tough, south London secondary school, a student informed her that she sounded like a squeaking rat. Clearly, it wasn't yet time for that singing career!

Instead, she moved to Atlanta and obtained a Masters degree from Emory University before working in management consulting in New York. After returning home to the UK, she said goodbye to corporate employment and trained to be a life coach. She promptly used the coaching skills on herself and for several years worked as a supply teacher while taking singing lessons, in the hope of one day being able to fulfil her childhood dream. During school lunch breaks she would sit in her car and run through her vocal exercises.

Shola has sung in Europe, the Middle East, Africa and the USA and was once a backing singer for Florence and the Machine. In 2016 she won the Jenny Seagrove public speaking award and is available internationally for speaking and training events. She also speaks at schools around the country on the subject of careers and life skills.

She lives in London and enjoys travel, Thai food, tennis, and rebounding.

Find out more or connect with Shola at **www.sholakaye.com**. Sign up to learn about events and courses, and to receive speaking tools, tips and more.

Email: **SpeakUpDiva@gmail.com**
Web: **www.SholaKaye.com**
Connect on Instagram:
www.instagram.com/speakuplikeadiva